*I was against Christianity
profoundly touched by the u
without basic human needs
night in 1977 until now, I have been filled with a great desire to serve God and my
people. This book is the story of my village and how God used the Corsons to help us
develop and change our community.*

—Benjo Paredes, leader of Sapecho and the Alto Beni, converted atheist,
founder of CENATEC and partner in the development of SIFAT

*Sarah Corson invites you into the heart of the life she and her family experienced
for two years in a corner of the world most of us know nothing about. Their
journey of faith among the Bolivian people as unconventional missionaries who
assimilated into the culture is a compelling read. This story will touch you with
God's love, compassion and provision…and maybe challenge you to boldly live
your faith as well!*

—Debbie and Michael W. Smith, Grammy and Dove Award-winning Songwriters

*The stories in Sarah's book are inspiring and gripping as the reader enters
the Bolivian culture, so different from western culture. She uses such creative
language that the reader cannot help but engage vicariously in the challenges of
living with the poor and seeking to minister to their needs.*

—Dr. Richard L. Stryker, Southeast District Superintendent North Alabama
Conference of the United Methodist Church

Sarah Corson's Risking Everything *will inspire a new generation of families
to press beyond their fears to see what lies ahead in God's plan for their lives.*

—Don Wise, Executive Producer/Developer of the Best-Selling
The Beginner's Bible

*Sarah Corson has told a great story of the wild adventure of following Christ
through Bolivia. As an international leader of Christian mission to God's
beloved poor and oppressed people, Sarah's story is an inspiration and a challenge
to all of us. Here is an engaging story about a fine Christian family on the road
in mission with Jesus.*

—Will Willimon, author and Bishop of the North Alabama Conference
of the United Methodist Church

RISKING EVERYTHING

Sarah Corson

One Family's Journey of Faith
in the Jungles of Bolivia

SIFAT
Lineville, Alabama

SIFAT Publications
A Division of SIFAT
Servants in Faith and Technology
2944 County Road, Lineville, Alabama 36266

Unless otherwise indicated, all Scripture quotations are taken
from *The New King James Version*. Copyright © 1979, 1980, 1982,
Thomas Nelson, Inc.

For information about special discounts for bulk purchases,
please contact SIFAT Special Sales
256-396-2015 or visit our Web site www.sifat.org

The SIFAT Speakers Program can bring the authors to your live
event. To book an event, contact us at 256-396-2017 or visit our
Web site www.sifat.org

Produced by Don Wise Productions, Inc.
Edited by Anne Severance
Map illustration by Dyla Corson

Printed in the United States of America.
10 9 8 7 6 5 4 3 2 1/ 1 2 3 4 5 6 7 8 9 10

ISBN: 978-0-9759666-1-7 (e-book)
ISBN: 978-0-9759666-2-4 hardcover
ISBN: 978-0-9759666-3-1 softcover

**To Ken Corson—
my husband, my friend**

This book could only have been written with his encouragement and help. From the time we lived this story 32 years ago, until today when we are finishing the manuscript, and all the years in between, Ken has been a true partner in the everyday living out of our lives and in the writing of this book.

We are two very different individuals; in fact, we are often opposites. He likes classical music; I like Southern Gospel songs. He likes pizza and submarines; I like turnip greens and cornbread. Through all the hurt and frustration such differences cause, we have learned how to forgive and forget, how to give each other space, and how to be there when needed, regardless of circumstances. We have learned that love is not just an emotion; love is a commitment. From the beginning we knew that it took three to get married. Christ must be the head of our home.

During the first week of our marriage, Ken proposed this principle for our life together: Our differences can give us a broader outlook, helping us to understand more of life. We will be complementary, instead of conflicting. Together, we can become more than the sum of what we could have been individually. Thank you, Keno, for making that a reality! I could never imagine a greater life on this earth…than this one in which I have been profoundly blessed by living it with you for the last 52 years!

Acknowledgments

In 1976, when we moved to Bolivia, Edgar Stevenson, then editor of the *Randolph Press* and John B. Stevenson, editor of the *Roanoke Leader*, our weekly county newspapers, asked us to write a column about life in Bolivia. For two years our columns ran in those papers. Writing that column disciplined me to record the details of our life as we lived it in the jungle. If we had not written it when it happened, we could never have remembered all those details years later. Thanks to those newspapers, we have a weekly record of the two years we spent in Bolivia. Those articles were the resource I used to fill in the details for this book.

Today, those two newspapers have merged to become the *Randolph Leader.* Though Edgar and John B. have passed on, we want to express our profound appreciation for their lives and for the life of the present editor, John W. Stevenson, who has given permission to use the excerpts from the articles in this book. These three men have been most helpful in our work both before and after the founding of SIFAT.

Many people have helped to make this book possible. Joe Patrick, then administrative assistant at SIFAT, spent many hours beyond the call of duty collecting the newspaper articles and putting them in useful order. Alicia Lockwood spent untold volunteer hours typing the articles into computer format. Linda

Hall Sullivan did proofreading for the book. Brenda Beasley did the first edit of this book and made it a much better volume. Jim and Linda Beasley loaned us their condo for a quiet place to write. We are very thankful to them all and to many others who have helped all the way back to 1978 in Bolivia, when Missionary Barbara Robison lent me her Underwood typewriter for a week to first type up the handwritten articles I had sent to the newspapers. Peggy Walker, my husband Ken, and our son Tom read the manuscript and gave very helpful suggestions.

During this last year of finishing this book, we became good friends with our publisher, Don Wise, his wife, Chris, and Anne Severance, our editor. Their friendship has become important in our lives. Being in close touch with Anne, often daily, by email has been a great blessing. She pointed out to me things that I took for granted, but might be confusing to the public in the cross-cultural missionary context so that I could clarify. She became a true friend while working through this book with me.

Many people gave me feedback on this book. Thank you to all who helped me—those mentioned and the many others not mentioned!

Sarah Corson
Wedowee, Alabama
July, 2010

Chris, Kathy, Tom and Karen before leaving for Bolivia

Table of Contents

Introduction

Someone was knocking at our door....

It was the postman with a letter from the Methodist bishop in Bolivia, inviting us to become pastors there! With no instant communication in 1976, we had been waiting for weeks for this invitation—ever since hearing Bob Caufield speak about his experiences as a missionary there, and expressing our interest in the work.

Ken and I were thrilled! Our whole family, including our four children—Chris, Kathy, Tommy and Karen, ages 15, 12, 11, and 10—would soon be moving from Alabama to the South American jungle, where the indigenous people lived in abject poverty.

We hugged each other and praised the Lord, then called the children in to tell them. "We have been invited to serve as pastors in Bolivia!" we exclaimed.

"Bolivia? What's it like?" Questions about our new home began to fly, thick and fast.

"Will I have new carpeting in my room like

I have now?" Kathy asked.

"Do they have Little League teams there?" Tommy wanted to know.

Karen was next. "Will everyone speak Spanish?"

Our fifteen-year-old, Chris, voiced his greatest concern. "But can I get my driver license down there"

Our ultimate destination would be the small village of Sapecho near the Alto Beni River, which is part of the headwaters that make up the Amazon drainage basin.

We had been told that nine homesteaders had built a small bamboo church and had requested a pastor from the Methodist Church many times. We were honored to be the first of any church to serve this village and surrounding area since the initial homesteaders settled this river valley in 1962.

We invite the reader to accompany us on our journey into the jungles of Bolivia. We will introduce you to some of the most beautiful, marginalized people who have ever lived and hope that you will understand their intense struggle to develop against incredible odds. We found that to know these people was to love them. The two years we lived with them became the greatest learning experience of our lives.

We hope that this journal will challenge you

to join us in helping to stop the tsunami of suffering, not only for the people of the Alto Beni, but for over half the people in our world.

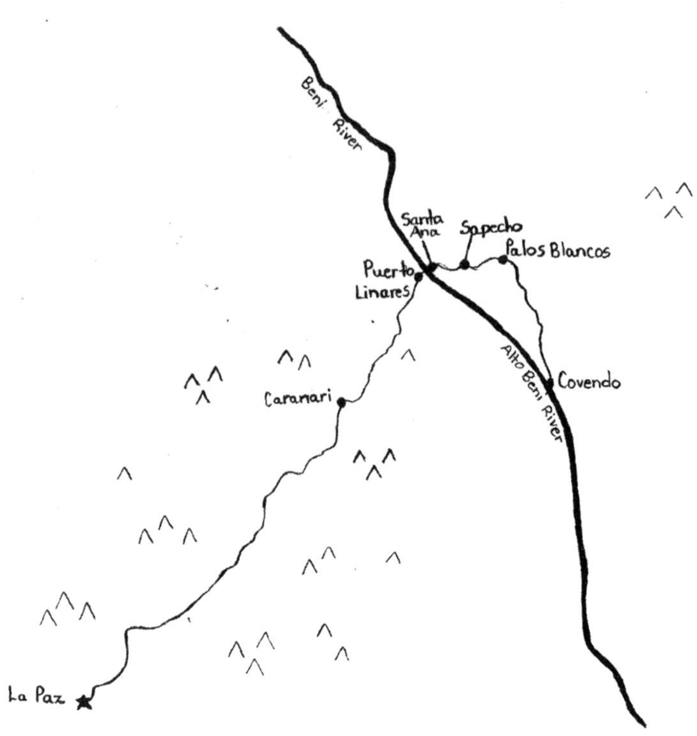

Simple map of the Alto Beni where most of the story in this book took place. The dark line is the Alto Beni/Beni River. The lighter line is Death Road, from La Paz down to Puerto Linares and Santa Ana on the river and across to Sapecho and on to Palos Blancos and Covendo where the road ended in the jungle.

(opposite page)
L to R: Ken, Tom, Chris, Kathy, Sarah and Karen after arriving in Bolivia

Chapter One

The New Pioneers

*We faced an unchanging paradox that was Bolivia
—a land of the greatest beauty one could possibly imagine,
coupled with some of the most severe suffering.*
—Ken Corson

We stepped off the plane at the airport on the Altiplano above La Paz. This city, one of Bolivia's two capitals, is situated in a bowl-shaped hole, scooped out of this high plain some 13,000 feet up in the Andes Mountains. We were eager to begin our two-year stint as pastors among the homesteaders in Sapecho, a small village in the Alto Beni region. Under the auspices of the Bolivian Methodists, we would pastor a little bamboo church, built by nine homesteading families. We—my husband Ken; our children—Chris, fifteen; Kathy, twelve; Tommy, eleven; and Karen, ten—and I would live among them, hopefully become one with them.

As leaders of the national Bolivian church met us and took Ken to retrieve our suitcases, the children and I almost fell into seats in the waiting room. At that high altitude the air was so thin we could hardly breathe. "Mommie, I'm sick..." groaned Tommy. *"Real* sick!"

I tried to steady him as we staggered toward a bathroom. The bathroom was located downstairs; we had to hang onto the handrail to keep from falling. Altitude sickness! We had been warned about that. After Tommy felt better, we found we could not even climb back up the steps without sitting down every few feet to catch our breath.

In the taxi leaving the airport, our driver zigzagged down the steep side of the mountain into La Paz, stopping long enough for us to take in the scenic beauty of the formidable Andes Mountains, and then to look below at the capital of Bolivia, filled with skyscrapers like any modern city. The city seemed caught in the embrace of the encircling mountains.

"How beautiful!" I gasped.

All around the business center and up the treacherous mountainsides, small houses, seemingly on top of each other, were wedged into every available space. These spoke forcefully of poverty. "Yes, Bolivia is very beautiful," Ken agreed. "But look at those children…it's their plight that concerns me."

In a tiny yard below us, three little children huddled under a poncho, shivering in the cold. From that moment on, we faced the unchanging paradox that was Bolivia….a land of the greatest beauty one could possibly imagine, coupled with some of the most severe suffering.

We knew that thousands of feet below, tropical vegetation grew lush and green. Deep rivers, like ribbons, curled through thickly forested valleys. Above us, towering, snow-crowned peaks pierced the incredibly blue sky, while here in the immediate vicinity of the high plain called the Altiplano, the wind whipped across barren land, unhindered by trees or undergrowth. It was indeed a study in contrasts.

Death Road desends down the Andes mountains with only one lane.

Down "The Road of Death"

Across the mountains and the valleys,
The Church of Jesus keeps right on a-marching!
Down the highways and mountain byways,
The Church of Jesus keeps right on a-going!
Christian, don't stop loving! Don't stop loving now!

—Translated from a Spanish chorus sung in Bolivia

After the church leaders gave us a two-week orientation to Bolivia—a whole new world—we were ready to travel down the Andes to our new home.

The leaders had explained that sixteen years earlier, a narrow road had been opened through the steep cliffs of the Andes to the Alto Beni. Today's TV documentary channels call it "Death Road." This road twists and turns on narrow ledges, dropping down some 13,000 feet over 200 miles to the rain forest below. Before the road was built, it was difficult to reach the tropics, where there was plenty of land and a better climate for farming. Now, however, because of overcrowded and poor conditions among the indigenous people on the high Altiplano, many who had never owned land quickly began to follow this road down the mountain, longing for the opportunity to make a home and cultivate a farm to support themselves. They often arrived with only the tools and material belongings they could carry on their backs.

Most of these people knew very little about farming in the tropics, but anything was better than working long hours in the tin mines for a pittance—never enough to buy adequate food for their families. Many of their children died of malnutrition, but the new road symbolized hope. Their bitter, harsh lives gave them the courage to leave the place of their birth and tackle an unknown jungle with only a machete.

Since the completion of the road, thousands have migrated to the Alto Beni region. More are still coming, seeking a place where hard labor and perseverance will enable their families to survive and prosper. We want to share the story of our sojourn with these hardy pioneers as we learned from them and tried to contribute something of value to their lives. It was truly an experience that changed the way we would understand life forever…for Ken and me, as well as for our children.

At 7:30 in the morning, we were at the bus station in La Paz, preparing to travel down the so-called "Most Dangerous Road in the World" to the Alto Beni.

For over a year we had waited for this day, and now it was here! Bob Caufield, director of the Methodist High School in the Alto Beni, had come up to escort us back down. He and Ken were busy hoisting the passengers' suitcases, boxes and goods wrapped in blankets to the man on top of the bus. When the top was loaded, we all began scrambling for our seats. It would be a long ride, ten to twelve hours they had told us, over the "Road of Death."

All seven of us—Ken and I, with our four children, along with Bob—settled down as the bus started climbing the rim which encircles La Paz. There were not enough seats, but the passengers obviously knew how to make do with whatever was available. Since there were many Aymaran "suitcases" in the aisles—beautifully woven blankets with everything wrapped inside—there were plenty of these bundles for the extra people to sit on.

Just as I was getting acquainted with Doña Severina, the Aymaran lady sitting on her bundle in the aisle at my side, the bus stopped. It started, went a few feet, choked and then stopped again. The bus had broken down…and we were still in La Paz!

As we rolled to a complete halt, vendors burst through the door of the bus. It was already very crowded inside, but the aggressive salespeople, most of whom were children, pushed past everyone, eight or ten of them at a time, all shouting their wares. "Bread!" called one. "Buy my fresh bread!" "Apples!" said another little girl. "Three apples for five pesos." Chewing gum, candy, crackers, cookies and glasses of some kind of drink were offered.

Still another child was holding two glasses, covered with saucers. "What do you have there?" I asked him. "Water with sugar and cinnamon," he replied, assuring me that the water was boiled— very important here, as much of the water carries parasites.

Some of the vendors stayed in the bus until it started and had actually gone a half block or so before they jumped out the door, departing as abruptly as they had entered.

The bus, still not running smoothly, chugged along until the driver came to a mechanic's shop. There, to our surprise, was the truck loaded with all our clothes, tools and household effects. The truck was supposed to have left La Paz three days earlier! After learning that it, too, had broken down, we resigned ourselves to the fact that we would be arriving at our new home with only one change of clothes, no pans to cook in and very little to set up housekeeping. Our bus was soon repaired, and we left La Paz with a farewell glance at our earthly belongings on the truck in the mechanic's shop.

For some time we continued to climb, then high over the city of La Paz, we rounded a curve and leveled off on a plateau. All along this road, we saw children or women serving as shepherds, watching over their sheep, llamas or cows. They, too, were dressed in colorful skirts and shawls and wore derby-like felt hats like the other Aymaran women we had seen.

As we rode along, Doña Severina introduced us to her husband sitting in the aisle in front of her. Their six-year-old son leaned against him while she held their two-year-old baby. They owned a restaurant in the Alto Beni along the riverside, they told us, and had been visiting his family in another part of Bolivia.

The winds that continually sweep the plateau had left only a few clumps of grass for the animals to forage. The colorfully dressed shepherdesses followed them, watching to assure that they would not stray too far.

On a high rise overlooking the plain below was a homestead. The house was made of mud and straw brick, which the natives call *adobe*. There were some shelters for the animals, too, but no trees. Here in this forsaken spot, some father and mother were trying to eke out a living for their children. When I glanced over to the other side of the road, I suddenly felt a little of their crushing hardship and sorrow, for there, side by side, were five little graves, neatly marked by homemade cement tombstones. *Oh, Señora,* my heart cried out to the Aymaran woman I did not know, *five of your little ones did not make it!*

Goat herder in the Andes Mountains

Around the next curve a boy of about ten was driving a few sheep and three llamas, his brightly colored woven cap around his ears. His llamas stood erect, looking proud and stately, perhaps much like the ancient Incas from whose flocks they descended. The boy smiled shyly as we went by, answering my greeting with a timid wave.

At least one made it, Señora. I thought back to the roadside graves. *I hope you have others too.*

"I hate to travel," Doña Severina broke in on my thoughts. As I looked out the window, I agreed with her completely. We had left the plateau and were descending the steepest mountainside I had ever seen. I held my breath while the bus zigzagged down the mountain. Each time we turned, I thought we could not possibly make the next sharp curve. We were at the bottom before I could respond. "Yes"—my voice was as shaky as my knees—"I guess I hate to travel too!"

But that mountain was only a pleasant little drive compared to what lay ahead. Bob pointed out to us on the far horizon a steep mountain peak, barely discernible at this distance. "The Alto Beni lies beyond that peak," he said. It was a simple statement, spoken calmly and as a matter of fact, which is the way Bob Caufield accepts everything. But the next eight hours were the most breathtaking hours I had ever spent...to that point in my life.

The Amazing Andes

I will always think of the Andes Mountains with great respect. Their steep sides, the sheer drop-offs to the river winding far below, are more than the human mind can comprehend. We witnessed view after view of the most tremendous beauty, but these could hardly register on my consciousness for the overwhelming fear of plunging over the edge of that little one-lane road, carved into the sides of the towering cliffs.

By 10:30 we came to a small settlement. The bus stopped for us to eat lunch in a rustic restaurant. "What's on the menu?" Bob asked.

"Today we have a choice of cow's tongue or cow's stomach," the owner replied. We left the meat and took a bowl of soup instead.

As we started our journey again, our fifteen-year-old son Chris asked Bob, "What do we do if we meet someone on the road?" Already the road was barely wide enough for one vehicle. Furthermore, there were never any side rails, only complete drops down, down, down. On the other side, sheer rock cliffs jutted into the sky above us.

"You'll see in a little while" was the only explanation Bob gave him.

And we did see! Very soon we met another bus lumbering up the mountain. Expecting a head-on collision, a little scream escaped my lips. When both vehicles finally stopped, they were bumper to bumper. On the right, I saw a high bank about a yard from the window of the bus. Above the heads of the people behind me, I could see a sharp curve out the back window. And then I glanced once—only once—out my window to the left. It appeared that there was only about a foot of ground between the bus and the drop-off to the river straight below—*far* below!

The driver of the bus facing us gestured wildly, motioning us to back up. *Impossible!* I thought. But to my horror, our driver, muttering under his breath, put the bus in reverse.

I did not see how he maneuvered the narrow, sharp curve because I could not force my eyes open. I was convinced that we had no alternative but to drop to our death. But when I opened my eyes, we were still on the narrow ledge, only now we were no more than two inches from the precipice. The other bus was inching its way along.

All public vehicles on this road were required to have an assistant to help the drivers negotiate the hard places in the road. Our assistant jumped out and began to call to the drivers in Spanish. "You move up...about a foot. Wait!" He held up one hand like a traffic cop, then motioned the other forward. "Now—*you*—just a few inches! Stop! Now you...."

This went on until, by some miracle, the two buses passed. This time I forced myself to watch. I am sure that if my finger had been between the two buses, it would have been smashed! We were that close. But then the other bus was gone, and we had the whole road to ourselves—all one lane of it.

It was then that I noticed that Doña Severina was sick. She was on her knees in the aisle, bending over her bundle. I put my hand on her forehead and tried to steady her, but she motioned toward the baby. Her two-year-old lay on the floor at her feet and as I glanced down at him, he vomited. She was too sick to help him.

After the encounter with the other bus, I had felt sick, too, but now there was no time for that. I picked up the crying baby. There was nothing with which to clean him, no baby wipes, no diaper. I just took him as he was. Soon he had quit crying and was asleep in my arms. Trying to console the sick woman and holding her baby occupied me for several hours. It was good for me to have something to do to keep my mind off the road we were traveling.

In the late evening we came to Caranavi,

a small dusty town where we stopped for a bottle of soda pop, called a *refresco*. Bob pointed out the peak we had seen early that morning, much nearer now. Gradually we approached and began our climb. At the summit, we looked out over a vast expanse of land—mountains, valleys, plains—a lush, green panorama. For the first time, we were seeing the distinct part of this world that was soon to become our home—the region of the Alto Beni. Doña Severina felt better now that she was nearly home again.

Here lived over 15,000 families, homesteaders who had braved the same dangerous road we had traveled, looking for hope and an opportunity to make a new life. Far beyond was the Beni River and somewhere on the other side, hidden in the jungle, was the tiny village of Sapecho.

It was a dream come true. Even though the past ten hours had been a nightmare—a beautiful nightmare, I must admit—now we had actually arrived in the Alto Beni. When the bus stopped at the end of the line at a little community called simply Kilometer 73, the dream felt real and good beneath our feet.

(opposite page)
L to R: Chris, visiting volunteer John, Karen, Andres, Tom, Kathy and Ken.
Our first little bamboo house in the Alto Beni is behind the Caufields's jeep.

Chapter Two

First Days in the Alto Beni

*The greatest heritage we can leave our children
is not an easy way of life, nor even a particularly long life,
but rather the ability to overcome the fear of
risking everything in order to follow God's call.*

Our first day in the Alto Beni had finally arrived.
Even though our village, Sapecho, was across the
river, ten miles farther into the jungle, at least we
would be living in our district. For now, we were

to stay near the Methodist missionaries, Bob and Rosa Caufield, until we could get a house built in Sapecho.

Two of the Caufields's children were still at home. Sixteen-year-old Steve was about the age of our Chris and ten-year-old Jennine was our Karen's age. When Steve and Jennine took us over to our new home, a little house made of bamboo cane belonging to the Methodist High School, we were not surprised to find that the Caufields had already furnished the house with basic necessities.

Around the high school, the houses had electricity for about three hours each night. There was an old kerosene refrigerator, which would freeze on only half the freezing unit. It acted tired, for every three or four days it would go off and rest for a day or two. Despite its problems, this "modern convenience" helped us to adjust gradually to the different way of life here. We were also blessed with the luxury of a little gas stove for cooking instead of having to resort to an open fire as did most of the people in this area.

Kilometer 73

After moving in, we toured the community

where we were to live temporarily. It was a center, not a town. There were the government offices in charge of homesteading, called the "colonization offices." Then there was a clinic with four rooms for patients, an intern, and a public health nurse, called a *sanitario,* who often served these frontier areas as doctor. Three little stores sold bread, candy, soft drinks and a few other items such as oatmeal and rice. And there was the high school, with several acres used to teach agriculture. This school, which the Caufields started, was the only high school for miles around.

The wife of one of the homesteaders prepared meals for all who reserved a plate in a little dirt-floored, open-air restaurant called a *pensión.* The menu was the same for everyone—usually a homemade soup and a plate of food that tasted good, but contained at least three starchy vegetables such as rice, potatoes, and *yucca,* or cooked bananas. Those who did not stop by to reserve a plate could eat only if there were leftovers. The meal cost fifty cents, and if one wanted a soft drink to go with the meal, an additional twenty-five cents.

One of the first residents we met at Kilometer 73 was the wild pig which the owners of the restaurant were raising as a pet. Wild pigs roamed free in the surrounding jungle, and the owners had caught this one as a baby. It was about eighteen inches tall with stiff bristles standing out all over. A long, thin snout was attached to a rotund body, perched on thin, spindly legs.

While waiting for our household goods to arrive, we ate three meals a day in this *pensión*. There was no electricity at the restaurant, so at night we ate by candlelight. One night in the semi-darkness, I felt something rubbing against my leg. I jumped, and we peered under the table to see the amiable wild pig, trying to make friends with us while we ate. It was a new experience for me, for I had never eaten in a restaurant where a wild pig wandered around, mingling with the dinner guests. This was only one of many new experiences.

Puerto Linares, Our Town

One day soon after we arrived, Rosa Caufield took us to buy groceries in the main town, Puerto Linares, situated along the bank of the Beni River. All along the riverbank indigenous people had parked their canoes, many of them dugouts made from hollowed-out trees. These canoes were loaded with bananas being brought to market.

Buying groceries in the main town, Puerto Linares,
situated along the bank of the Upper Beni River.

The one dirt road through the middle of town was crowded with trucks and truckers who had come to purchase and haul the bananas back up to La Paz. The whole town was only two blocks long, with several *pensiónes,* a few dry goods stores, a vegetable stand, two grocery stores and a pool hall. In the grocery stores, a dozen or more burlap sacks stood, full and open, ready for sale. A clerk would measure out the desired amount of macaroni, spaghetti, dry hominy, corn meal, flour or rice. Vegetable stands offered cabbage, carrots, potatoes, bananas and an occasional pumpkin. Since the stores had no paper or plastic bags, the shoppers brought their own, usually made of cloth, to carry their purchases home.

On the way back, we stopped by the open-air meat market. Hanging from two meat hooks was the cow they had butchered that morning. It was a gory sight—the hooves, tail and head lying on the floor! The owner cut off whatever piece we asked for, weighed it and sold it to us for $1.30 a kilo, approximately 62 cents a pound. Sirloin or soup bones—all sold for the same price. Unfortunately for our children, there was no hamburger unless one ground it at home.

After we finished buying groceries, we stopped by the *pensión* owned by the family who had made the bus trip with us from La Paz. The "restaurant" was a tiny room on stilts, suspended over the Beni River. At the back of the room, Doña Severina cooked over little kerosene burners. Spotting us as we entered, she wiped her hands on her apron and pushed past stacks of soft drink cases to greet us.

We bought a cup of hot chocolate, made from the chocolate which was grown there without processing and mixed with sugar and water, because milk was not available. The unprocessed chocolate was very strong, yet it was good in its own way.

While we enjoyed our drink, Doña Severina's two-year-old baby came up to us, clicked his heels and saluted as he had seen the officers and men do every day at the Navy post next door. Bolivia was a military government at that time and, though there was no outlet to the sea, their Navy patrolled the rivers. The little boy remembered that I had held him coming down that road when he was sick, and he climbed up in my lap again while we drank our hot chocolate.

Children have always melted my heart, and I suddenly thought of Jesus, who welcomed the little ones and did not send them away. "Of such are the kingdom of heaven," and it was our mission to help bring more of His kingdom here to the Alto Beni.

Daily Life in the Alto Beni

A few days passed as we struggled to adjust to our new lifestyle. It seemed that our whole day was consumed with trying to keep ourselves clean and fed. The heat exhausted us more than the work. Every day there was the same monotonous menu—carrots and cabbage for vegetables, with rice, potatoes or macaroni, and on butchering days, beef (when we had time to go to market).

We planted a small garden even though we expected to be moving about the time it began to produce. All of us soon grew tired of carrots and cabbage, so the children went out daily to weed the garden and see how the green beans, okra and squash were doing. The rainy season had begun, and with the hot sun between showers, our crops grew fast indeed.

Kathy and Karen wash dishes in our open-air kitchen under an avocado tree.
To the left is a hand-operated washing machine, which we soon
discarded for the cooler task of washing in the river.

In the heat and humidity, bugs descended on us by the thousands. There was a tiny bug about the size of a pinpoint that kept us itching day and night. These little bugs even came through the mosquito nets we slept under. Although the nets didn't keep all the bugs out, they protected us from the vampire bats that flew in through cracks in the bamboo walls at night and pierced the veins of sleeping people with their razor-sharp teeth!

Since there was no source of safe drinking water, we boiled it in the big pot we had brought for that purpose. What we had not anticipated was that, in this heat, it would take fourteen to sixteen hours for the water to cool to room temperature. Not only that, but we didn't have a place to store the water except in the same pot, so we couldn't boil more till we emptied this one. Often we were so thirsty we would drink the boiled water hot—like coffee. In the extreme heat, lack of cold drinking water didn't help the depression that began to descend upon us. We could see that, under these circumstances, it was going to be hard to keep from yelling at one another, much less remain cheerful.

During this difficult time, a familiar Scripture frequently came to mind: "I can do all things through Christ who strengthens me" (Phil. 4:13). Those words gave us the ability to keep forgiving each other for little irritations and to look beyond the difficulties in this culture that sometimes seemed overwhelming. The verse also helped us to focus on God's call to become one of these people and to let His love flow through us to all we met.

One day, when the water was almost cool

enough to taste like drinking water, I called the whole family together. We gathered around the big pot and reached for the dipper.

Suddenly Kathy squealed, "There's a frog in the water!"

We were so thirsty, we shooed the frog out and drank anyway. We were fast becoming accustomed to the little creatures. Our house was filled with frogs, the kind that jump halfway up a wall and cling to it. But we didn't mind them when they stayed out of our water and food because they ate the mosquitoes and sang to us at night around our beds.

◊

By noon each day, the heat was almost unbearable. Our little house—18' x 24'—with its tin roof, was so hot we could barely breathe. One of the first days we were there, Steve and Jennine came over to take us to a little river nearby to do our wash. At noon—when it is too hot to do anything else—was the perfect time.

The Suapi River ran down behind our house. The water was waist-deep, with rocks jutting out, where the women scrubbed their clothes. Unlike the Beni River two miles below, the Suapi was clear and clean to the eye, though of course we could not drink it without boiling it first. We took our baths here and carried our water for cooking from this river too. It was the community's only source of water, and we were fortunate that it was so near.

In the afternoon, the heat was less intense, and we were able to continue with our other work. Chris and Tommy were helping Ken build a new outhouse because the old one was falling in when we arrived. It took us almost a month to be able to deal adequately with the circumstances of daily life. But these inconveniences were minor compared to the stark reality that faces every homesteader in the Alto Beni—serious injury with limited medical care, lack of food and premature death.

"Not Many of Us Live to Be Old."

One of Ken's jobs during our tenure was to help develop better ways of producing protein, for the diet of the people was usually lacking in this vital element. Some years ago, there had been fish in abundance in the Suapi River, but many of the new homesteaders, being desperate for food until they could get established, and lacking hooks and proper fishing gear, had used dynamite to fish for their families. The poor and the uneducated, not realizing how this method would affect the ecology, adopted this technique and used it frequently. Therefore, the fish left in the Suapi were very small. Even though there was a law against fishing with dynamite in Bolivia, there was no one to enforce the law.

On one of our first days at Kilometer 73, our son Tommy followed a truckload of workers hauling rice hulls to the high school to mulch the school's fruit trees. He heard the dynamite blast down on the river. We heard it from the house, too, but it was such a common occurrence that we didn't think much about it. A few minutes later, after the farm workers had left and Tommy was walking home alone, he heard a groan and suddenly a man appeared, struggling up the path from the river.

To our son's dismay, he saw that half the man's hand was blown off and he was desperately trying to reach the clinic a half-mile away. Since this poor fellow was in a state of shock, Tommy, horrified by the bloody pulp of a hand and the man's groans, walked with him, for there was no transportation and he was losing blood.

Nearing our house, Tommy yelled for help. When we saw the man's condition, we felt shocked and helpless too. With no car or other transportation available, all I could think to do was to let him smell some ammonia we had to keep him from fainting. *"Gracias, gracias,"* the man muttered between groans. His eyes were set and glazed, and he appeared not to comprehend what had happened. It was fortunate that the clinic was so near the site of the accident.

The next day the same thing happened to a man twenty kilometers away; he had to walk the whole distance to the clinic with half his hand blown off. When we mentioned it to the neighbors, they just shrugged. "Too bad. But that's the way of life here...accidents...sickness. Not many of us live to be old." There were so few doctors and so few roads and vehicles to take people to the doctors when they were hurt or sick.

Later that week, we visited the patients in the clinic, heard their stories of their fight against sickness and death, talked and prayed with them. But when we came to one young boy's bed, he just stared at us as though he did not understand a word we were saying. He didn't appear to be sick. He just looked frightened and stared at us blankly. *He must be one of the indigenous people who do not understand Spanish,* I thought, so I put my hand on his shoulder, spoke a few words of sympathy and moved on.

◊

Since the next day was Sunday, we borrowed a jeep and crossed the Beni River on the ferry to attend church service in Sapecho. Late that afternoon as we drove off the ferry coming back, the ambulance from the clinic was waiting to board. As we passed, I caught a glimpse of the mother, weeping by the side of a body covered in a sheet.

We learned that it was the fifteen-year-old boy we had spoken to in the hospital. He was one of the students in the high school. They had brought him to the hospital after he had fallen and hit his head on something. Since the blow, he had not spoken a word, only stared. His brain must have been severely damaged. Sadly, the clinic was not equipped to help him.

I couldn't forget that mother in the ambulance, weeping beside the body of her teenage son. What if that were *my* son? One little fall…and just like that, he is dead! To receive the proper medical help for such injuries would take ten to twelve hours of rough riding over that long, precarious road. If one were seriously ill, he might die before arriving. For a split second a seed of fear lodged in my heart….

I had observed that people's attitude toward death in the Alto Beni was quite different from ours. They loved their children as much as we loved ours, but death was so much more common, especially among children who had parasites and who did not have enough protein in their diet. Even the little children accepted death as a normal part of life; there were so many orphans. These children were accustomed to seeing others, like themselves, deprived of their parents. But for me, the idea of an early demise—especially in the case of children—was new, and getting used to the ever-present reality of death depressed me even more.

Risking Everything

One night, during our first month, everything came to a climax for me. We had all gone to sleep, when, in the middle of the night,

Karen, our youngest, who was sleeping on the top bunk bed above her sister Kathy, suddenly began to scream.

Our little living room served also as dining room and bedrooms, so we were separated from the girls only by a straw mat, which we had hung up to create a provisional wall. But it was dark and we were still unaccustomed to the house.

When we heard Karen's piercing scream, Ken and I both jumped up, but we got tangled in the mosquito netting and then the straw mat. We stumbled in the dark, for there was no electricity that late and we couldn't find a match for the candle. While Ken searched for a light, I rushed toward Karen's bed. As I reached her side, she became hysterical and either jumped or fell from the top bunk, slipping through my fingers. She hit a chair and then the floor and lay there screaming and writhing at my feet.

All the gruesome events of the past week flooded my consciousness. I feared that Karen's neck or her back might be broken. I saw that dangerous twelve-hour-long road we'd have to travel before we could get any real medical help. I saw that mother weeping beside the lifeless body of her son; I saw the man with the half-blown-off hand. I saw a vast throng of people in a place called the Alto Beni, where few lived to be old. Mentally I was screaming out in anguish, but my only thought remained unexpressed: *What have we done? Have we brought our children to this lonely, forsaken place to die?*

In a flash, I felt the presence of Jesus, and His answer broke over me in such a forceful way that I knew all over again that we had done the right thing in coming here. As I knelt there, trying to calm my daughter, even before Ken found the light and even before I knew how badly she was hurt, the realization came to me that there is more than one way to die. We will all die physically. But if we are afraid to follow God, if we are afraid to step out into the unknown when He calls us, then we can die mentally and spiritually while still existing physically.

Oh, Karen! my heart cried out to her. *If we had been afraid to do what we knew we should do, if we had stayed in our comfortable situation at home and not dared to risk the lives of all of us here, we would have dried up and died in another way.* I knew in that moment that God was reminding me that it is far better to die physically than spiritually.

Ken found a match and lit the candle. It

was only a nightmare, and even though Karen was slightly bruised from her fall, she was over it in a few days. But the incident had made me come to grips—not with the fear of my own death; I had passed that long ago—but with the fear of harm to our children. After that night I experienced a new freedom in our daily life, and much of the depression of those first days was gone.

For in that moment after Karen's fall, it came to me so positively that the greatest heritage we can leave our children is not an easy way of life, nor even a particularly long life, but rather the ability to overcome the fear of risking everything in order to follow God's call.

(opposite page)
Sarah, Karen, Jennine Caufield, and a homesteader neighbor, washing clothes in the cool stream.

Chapter Three

Clean Water for Christmas

Rarely, before coming to live in the Alto Beni alongside some of the poorest people in the world, had we known how to appreciate the simplest and most basic of God's blessings. Take water, for example.

At first I was somewhat repulsed by the number of dirty people here—adults as well as children. Even the church leaders often wore soiled clothing to services. But after living here awhile, I understood why. These people worked so hard in the fields to get food for their families that sometimes there were just not enough daylight hours to carry water too. Each drop was so precious to those who lived any distance from a stream. I soon found myself wearing clothes longer than I would have in the States because the time and energy to keep them clean just didn't always exist under these conditions.

Back in Alabama, our children's health teachers had drilled them on the need for cleanliness. That helped me now, for our children were willing to do the laundry by hand without complaining because they wanted clean clothes to wear. Tommy, especially, was always ready to pitch in until the last garment was finished. Kathy and Karen joined the other girls their age in contests to see who could get their families' wash the cleanest. Even now, Kathy and Karen can get stains out of clothing better than I.

So, on another hot day in the Alto Beni, after our lunch of cabbage and carrot stew, all our family took our dirty clothes down to the Suapi River. Others, who had arrived ahead of us, were already at work. Wading out waist-deep in the river to the rocks, we joined them, cooling off while we worked.

It was also a good time to get acquainted with the homesteaders living around us. One woman pointed far up the steep mountain on the other side of the river to a little thatched-roof hut in a clearing, surrounded by banana plants. She told us that this was her home, at least a half-hour's walk from the river.

When she finished washing her clothes, she spread them on the rocks to dry, bathed herself and then washed her long hair. She waited patiently another half-hour until her clothes were dry. Gathering them up, she wrapped them in her blanket, tied the load on her back and waved good-bye as she started up the steep jungle trail to her home. It was sobering to think that all the water she used each day had to be carried up that trail.

Carrying water was one of the most time-consuming tasks for the women of this area. Yet the people would have been happy to walk long distances if the water were only safe to drink. But it was not safe. Even though the water in the Suapi River was clear, we knew that it was infested with many types of microscopic parasites. If it were not boiled properly before drinking, one risked the possibility of becoming sick. That is why most people drank as little water as possible. Instead, they drank hot teas brewed from the leaves of avocado and other trees. They also boiled overripe bananas in water until the fruit liquefied, making a tasty hot drink, sweetened without sugar.

Señor Ortiz, a successful homesteader, told us he was ready to sell out and move back to La Paz because of the lack of safe water on his farm. "For fifteen years we've carried water and tried to keep it boiled," he said, "but the problem has just about got me beat."

These homesteaders cooked over an open fire. When water was boiled in that way, it tasted like smoke or ashes—somewhat like barbequed water. Many of the children disliked the taste and wouldn't drink it. So they slipped out to the streams and drank the cool, polluted water instead; many got sick. As a result three of Mr. Ortiz's eight children had died. To me, this was devastating.

The Water Project

Bob and Rosa Caufield had initiated a project to bring water to the community at Kilometer 73 around the location of the high school. Such a project was one of the best ways to inspire a community to work together since clean water was a pressing need they all shared.

People from five nations helped the community at Kilometer 73 get clean water. Above, a Bolivian homesteader and two volunteers—one from the U.S. and one from Holland—work together.

When the project was completed, there would be water for the hospital, the school and several community faucets for the people. Though there would not be enough to last all day, they hoped to have water in the morning, an hour or two at noon and then again in the evening.

The entire neighborhood worked together, the homesteaders donating their labor. An organization from Germany, called "Bread for the World," gave money for the pipes and helped with the planning. Volunteers from Holland came to offer their services. Bob Caufield and his American visitors worked many long hours a day on the project. Ms. Nely, a widow from Argentina, who was the secretary for the high school, hospital and homestead offices, served as coordinator. She wrote notices and then walked many miles to deliver them to let each homesteader know when it was his turn to work. Imagine! People from five nations working together to bring safe water to this little community!

One of the most exciting events we attended after coming to the Alto Beni was the inauguration of this water system. The people in the community climbed high up the mountain to the spring, which was the source of their water supply. The leaders and many of those who had helped with the project gave speeches of gratitude.

Afterward, the whole community walked

down the hill to the holding tank and, with much ceremony, opened the faucet. Cheers went up as we heard the precious liquid begin trickling into the tank. This was followed by more speeches, after which the group walked farther down the hill and across the Suapi on a swinging bridge to the school dining room.

When everyone was gathered in the room, along with some Bolivian officials and leaders from the groups who had helped, a prayer of thanksgiving was offered. Then Ms. Nely opened the faucet and all of us watched as the water came rushing out. Cups were passed around and, for the first time, the community at Kilometer 73 all drank together—safe water that did not have to be boiled first!

This was a day of great celebration. These homesteaders knew beyond doubt that water was one of the greatest blessings they could have. With Christmas approaching, the people in the school and in this little community knew that the water would be a tremendous gift for everyone.

Andres, Our Neighbor

Next door to our little "borrowed" house on the high school property was a bamboo, one-room hut with a dirt floor. This hut was the home of Andres, a twenty-year-old Aymaran young man, struggling to get through high school. He was now in the eleventh grade.

Andres's parents had abandoned him at an early age. The problems of their lives were so great that they had given him away to neighbors, who took him in return for the work he could do for them even as a child.

When he was fifteen, Andres hired out to a homesteader in the Alto Beni. He worked hard and received little pay except his food and a straw mat to sleep on. The farmer he worked for had a quarrel with a neighbor, and one night when the neighbor was drinking, he borrowed a gun and knocked on the farmer's door. Since Andres slept near the door, he answered the knock.

With only the light from the moon to see by, the drunken man thought Andres was the owner of the farm. He shot him and fled. The owner was so afraid, he came running and locked the door, leaving Andres wounded outside. The farmer was not hurt. In his place, lay fifteen-year-old Andres with a bullet through his hip.

For a month, Andres lay in the little clinic

at Kilometer 73. His wound became infected and he almost died. Finally, he was sent up that rugged road to La Paz. For two more months, he lay at the point of death. But he recovered.

Andres finished telling us this story in answer to our question as to why he had a slight limp when he walked. "By all rights I should be dead," he said, "but God helped me through it. I know He has a reason for my being alive. I don't know what it is yet, but I must get all the education I can to be prepared."

With Andres's reputation for working hard, he received maximum wages. In the Alto Beni, that was a quarter an hour. He worked during the summer vacation to try to save enough to pay his tuition, room and board in the high school during the year. But it was never enough. And since he had no place to cook, he had been eating only bread or whatever he could buy cheaply in the stores.

Our son Chris, who had become friends with Andres, asked if we could get him a little kerosene burner for Christmas so he could at least cook himself a hot meal at night. We planned to do that, but there were no small stoves available in the little town near us.

Andres shows Chris and Kathy how to dry cacao for chocolate.

On Christmas Eve, we had scheduled a Christmas drama in the Puerto Linares church, where we were helping the Caufields. Andres was chosen to play the part of Joseph.

I was behind the scenes with the young people who were waiting their turn to go onstage. While we waited, I told Andres that we were sorry we had been unable to get his Christmas present, but we would buy him a little burner as soon as we could find one. To my surprise he burst into tears. I had never seen Andres cry like that before…a twenty-year-old, sobbing great, deep sobs.

It was five minutes before we could get him calmed down, just in time for him to go onstage. Ken was directing the service that night and if someone had not requested him to lead an extra song, there would have been a weeping Joseph in the drama. As it was, there was a red-eyed Joseph.

After the service was over and we were all home again, Andres asked us to excuse his outburst. "My own parents never gave me anything," he explained. "So when strangers who have only known me a month offer to do something like this for me, I just cannot believe it." The little stove only cost ten dollars, but it was a life-changing gift for Andres.

We had not realized how hungry Andres had been at times as he tried to save his money for school. So we invited him to start eating with us each day. He became like an "adopted" member of our family. He knew that we didn't want money for his meals, but when he came in from a hard day's work in the fields, he always came right over to see if there was something he could do to help Ken.

When we camped out a week over in Sapecho to hold a Bible School, Andres gave up his week's earnings to go with us and teach the class of eight-, nine-, and ten-year-olds. We were impressed by his patience and his ability as a teacher.

Andres was just one of our neighbors at Kilometer 73; his story, one of hundreds we could tell of the people who were struggling against great odds to make a contribution to the development of the Alto Beni…to their world.

Bolivian girls help Karen (with puppy) and Kathy read the Spanish drama in the sanctuary of the church in Puerto Linares

Christmas in the Alto Beni

In the Alto Beni region of Bolivia, Christmas is celebrated by a special service at church. But it is very quietly observed, and few presents, if any, are exchanged. As was their custom, Bob and Rosa Caufield invited all of those working in development of the Alto Beni for a Christmas supper.

After the meal, we sat in their living room and went around the circle, each sharing a memory of a Christmas which had been meaningful in the past. Ms. Nely, secretary for all the offices in the area, had come with her husband from Argentina seventeen years before, when the government of Bolivia had first sent engineers to survey the newly accessible lands of the Alto Beni. Her husband was in exile in Bolivia because he had been on the wrong political side in his native Argentina. He had died in the Alto Beni and was buried there. Ms. Nely, his widow, had stayed on, a big help to the school, the clinic and the government offices.

Now as she was approaching her elderly years, she looked back over her past and shared with us the memory of one Christmas long ago in Argentina. As a young bride, she had gone with her husband to his home. She described the merry-making, the parties and the drinking with her new relatives in Buenos Aires. When Christmas morning dawned, their hang-overs were so bad that they spent most of the day in bed. "It left me empty," Ms. Nely shared with us, "and wondering if Christmas was really worth it."

Then she told us about her first Christmas as a Christian five years before. Jesus had become real to her through the Caufields, and that year the holiday was spent in acts of kindness as she thought of ways to bless her neighbors. She gave a party for the children of the poorer homesteaders, which she has continued every year. Ms. Nely concluded by saying that she had discovered the real meaning of Christmas, but only regretted not finding it sooner.

Dan, a twenty-two-year-old who had grown up in Africa with his missionary parents, spoke next. He was visiting the Caufields for a month. He told of one Christmas Eve when he and some other men had worked late, laying a pipeline on the edge of the Sahara Desert. Toward evening, on the way home in their jeep, a terrible windstorm had blown up, covering them with a thick cloud of swirling sand. They could not see which way to go and lost their sense of direction. Then they realized that if one sat on top of the jeep, he could spot the markers to guide them. Dan told how he had felt the presence of Jesus with him that Christmas Eve as he sat on top of the jeep, guiding the driver by knocks on the roof as they traveled through the sandstorm safely home.

Others spoke of a Christmas in Bolivia, or

in Holland, or New York, or Alabama. Though the stories were very different, all of them had one thing in common. No one remembered a Christmas with beautiful gifts or extravagant material things as being the most memorable. In the end, the memories that stood out to us were those in which we had shared with other people or others had shared with us.

The wife of a German Peace Corps worker, involved in helping bring clean drinking water to remote villages, recalled the Christmas of 1944 when American planes were approaching her home in Berlin on one side and Russian tanks on the other. She was a teenager that night as she huddled in the basement with a group of friends and sang Christmas carols by the light of one small candle. Later, as bombs started exploding around them, they blew out the candle and sat in darkness, quietly singing, "Silent Night, Holy Night."

"We were singing in German," she said, "but it was the same song you just sang in Spanish." (*And the same one my family is singing in English in Alabama tonight,* I thought to myself.) Tears rolled down her cheeks as she remembered that long-ago Christmas. With a final burst of emotion, she said vehemently, though so quietly we had to strain to hear her, "I don't hate Americans! I don't hate Russians! But I hate war!"

Ken and I told about our first Christmas together in Cuba. We had adopted a nine-year-old Cuban girl named Isabel, who needed a home. She had begged us to kill our little pet pig and cook it for Christmas Eve supper as the Cubans who could afford it did. So we killed the pig for Isabel. Soon the meal was ready—a whole roast pig in the center of the table. But that evening, Isabel was taken from us by her relatives. When suppertime came, Ken and I could not eat a bite. I could only look at the pig and cry.

Ken had an idea. He hurried off to look for all the other people in Santa Barbara who did not have extended familes that night. He found a single mother with three children and brought them to our home. In the village bar, he found a young man who was trying to drown his sorrow in rum, for his wife had left him the week before. Ken gathered others and brought them all to our home. As we shared the meaning of this season with them, I forgot all about our homesickness for Alabama and our loneliness for Isabel.

When we left the Caufields's house that Christmas night, we walked home under the stars—the Southern Cross instead of the North Star—more aware than ever that we were part of a much larger group than we could imagine. There are so many precious people from all over the world who also love and worship the same Christ of Christmas.

(opposite page)
Santa Ana, a picturesque, sleepy little village on the Sapecho side of the
Alto Beni River. You can see dugout canoes at the river's edge.

Chapter Four

Struggle in Sapecho

*If you want to be part of God's work to stop some of this suffering,
you have to do what you can, and what you can't do,
you must leave in His hands.*

—Mr. Barber, Retired Missionary

For two days Ken and Chris had been in Sapecho, working on our new house with help from the *hermanos* (brothers) of the church. Now it was time for me to cross the river and join them. I was eager to see what progress had been made.

Our eleven-year-old Tommy insisted on going with me, our newly acquired baby monkey, Kiki Dee, riding on his shoulder. Leaving the girls with the Caufields, we started out early and walked the two miles to our little port town, Puerto Linares. There, for ten cents each, we hired a dug-out canoe taxi to take us across the Beni River. They didn't charge for the monkey.

We sometimes waited all day for transportation in Sapecho. This was the way most people traveled unless they had a *mobilidad*.

On the opposite side of the river, Port Santa Ana—a little village composed of a cluster of thatched-roof bamboo huts—already looked hot and desolate in the morning sun. Two of the residents had opened their doors to invite passersby to stop in for a refreshing drink, served at tables in the front room. Outside one of these huts, written in a universal language, was the only sign in the whole village: "Coca Cola."

Tommy and I sat down to wait for a truck going into Sapecho. Once or twice a day, a beat-up old pick-up went from Port Santa Ana to Sapecho and on beyond to take passengers. But this morning the *Servicio Rapido* (Rapid Service, as the truck was called) was slow in coming. We had hoped for a big truck loaded with merchandise, but our hopes were in vain. So all morning we sat on some lumber out in front of the shipyard, waiting.

Actually it was a boat-yard, for the boats that travel the Beni are seldom more than thirty-five feet long. Two men and a woman with a baby tied on her back were also waiting to go to Sapecho. The woman, whose baby was fretful, kept walking him up and down the road. When the little one finally slept, she sat down beside us. She told us that the child had been quite sick and yesterday she had brought him to the doctor at Kilometer 73. This morning he was better and she was trying to return to her home in Sapecho, but after waiting in this hot sun, the baby's fever was rising again.

Kiki Dee was suffering from the heat, too, not to mention Tommy and me. And then we heard the ferry coming, bringing a truck. A group of people gathered. When the vehicle finally drove off the ferry and stopped, we all crowded around. "Sapecho?" we asked. "Aren't you going on to Sapecho?"

The driver merely shrugged. "I don't know. I'll get my orders from the captain of the Navy here. I've been sent to pick up a load of mahogany. Maybe it's here, maybe in Sapecho…I don't know."

The captain was eating lunch, so the truck driver waited with us. Afterwards, while the captain rested, we waited some more. After an hour he came out to say that the wood was a kilometer inland. Only one kilometer…and Sapecho was sixteen kilometers! It looked as if there would be no transportation that day.

Tommy and I could re-cross the river and walk the two miles back home. But what about the woman with the sick baby? "This is why we don't bring our sick children to the doctor more often," she explained. "Sometimes they get worse, having to wait so long in this heat."

About 2 P.M. the *Servicio Rápido* came and we were on our way to Sapecho. It was 3 P.M. when we arrived. We had left home at 9 o'clock in the morning. The sixteen-kilometer trip (about ten miles) had taken us six hours!

When we took this assignment in Bolivia, Ken and I had known it would not be easy. As we were getting ready to move to our more permanent home, the farthest Methodist outpost in this area, little things like lack of transportation consumed our days. We were learning how the people daily lived with frustration.

After spending a day that felt wasted to me, I asked myself, *How far should we go in accepting the poverty of the people we have come to serve? Are we accomplishing anything by losing so much time in order to live on their level?* Little did I know that my ability to accept this way of life was about to be tried to the limit. The experience waiting for me in Sapecho would plunge me into the blackest night of depression yet.

A Miracle for Marcos?

After six hours of waiting and riding, Tommy, the monkey and I arrived in Sapecho.

After jumping down from the back of the truck, we eagerly started down the trail to meet Ken and Chris, who were helping the *hermanos* of the church build our new house.

Before we had reached the work site,

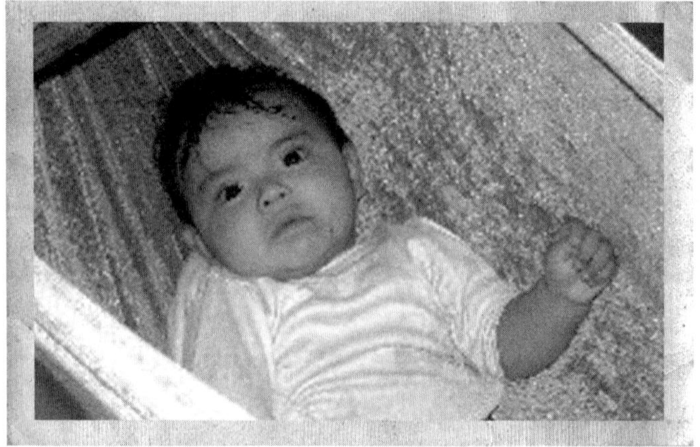

Baby Marcos in his handmade hammock

however, we were stopped by an urgent cry. Coming up the road was Señora Ramirez with her baby, little Marcos, on her back, the customary way of carrying small children. Marcos had been at the point of death when we had camped out over here to teach the Bible school several weeks ago, but we thought he had recovered.

"Marcos is sick again," Señora Ramirez called out to us. "Oh, I'm so afraid! What should I do? Please help us!"

We saw that the lively, alert little Marcos, whom we had learned to love, was indeed sick. His laughing brown eyes seemed lifeless today, and he whimpered in the hot sun. Tears streamed down Señora Ramirez's face as she repeated, "I'm so afraid. This is the only boy I have. My other four children are girls. Oh, I want to raise him! Do you think he will die, *Hermana*?" She called me by the affectionate term, meaning "sister," which the Bolivians use among fellow Christians.

"Hermana," I replied, "you must take this baby to the doctor at Kilometer 73. We still have a house there. You can sleep in our house tonight."

She agreed immediately. I talked to Ken briefly, had time for only a glance at the new house, and then returned to the road to wait for a truck to Kilometer 73 to accompany Señora Ramirez and her baby to the doctor.

But no truck came. Night came instead. Ken, Chris and Tommy quit work and joined us, waiting for transportation. When we were sure there was no hope of getting out of Sapecho that night, Señora Ramirez returned to her home to await the dawn. "Maybe supply trucks will come in the early morning," she said. "I'll go with you then."

Ken, our boys, Chris and Tommy, Kiki Dee and I returned to sleep on the eight-inch-wide benches in the church. We were tired, hungry and frustrated from our futile search for transportation. Our girls, Kathy and Karen, were expecting us home, but we were thankful that they were safe with Bob and Rosa Caufield. When a neighbor brought us a little cake of cornmeal mush, boiled in a corn shuck, we accepted it gratefully.

At daylight we were out on the road again, waiting for a truck. By 7 A.M. we heard one coming. When it stopped, we climbed on back, joining about forty other passengers. Señora Ramirez was there with Marcos wrapped in a blanket tied on her back. "He was so sick, *Hermana*," she sobbed. "All night I thought he would die. But he's alive and we have *mobilidad!*" she exclaimed, again using the Spanish word that means transportation of any kind.

I felt that the truck driver should have made room for the mother and her sick baby in the cab, but only those with more prestige were allowed to sit in front. At least I was glad that she had wrapped Marcos well, for the early morning air was chilly. We hung onto the side of the truck and bounced over rough roads—fourteen, fifteen, then sixteen kilometers. Arriving in Port Santa Ana, the truck stopped to wait for the ferry. Only two miles across the river to the little clinic and our home!

"*Hermana,* Marcos jumped. Look at him. Is he all right?" Señora Ramirez asked with fear in her eyes as she tried to see him over her shoulder. "Oh,

Hermana, have we come in vain?"

Quickly she untied the blanket that held him to her back and I took him in my arms. He was dying. Ken rushed over and gave him artificial respiration, but it was too late. "Yes, *Hermana,* I'm afraid we have come in vain."

The truck driver was at the side, collecting the fares. "Fifty cents each." Surely he could see the dying baby and his grief-stricken mother, but his attitude was like that of the other passengers. "Too bad…but it happens every day to the babies."

Bolivia has one of the highest infant mortality rates in our hemisphere. But to the mothers of those babies, the statistics would hurt just as badly if theirs were the only one. And I, who had only known Marcos a month, had come to love him. In my mind I re-lived those moments when I visited his home. Always, he had held out his little arms to me with laughing, happy eyes.

"Let's go back to Sapecho, *Hermana.* No need to go on now," Señora Ramirez said, weeping quietly at my side.

How I wanted to go home to my girls, but I could not leave her. Ken took the boys and went to see about our daughters, and I turned back toward Sapecho with Señora Ramirez. For once, there was a truck just coming up from the ferry. This time the truck driver noticed the little dead body we were holding and offered us the seat in the cab. We took it, though we didn't need it now. It was too late for Marcos.

That was one of the longest, saddest days of my life. When we got out of the truck at the Ramirez home, the husband came running to us, his arms outstretched. I put the little bundle in them. There was nothing to say. "Don't leave us, *Hermana,*" he said. "Don't leave us now."

Since there were no funeral homes in Sapecho, all morning the father worked, building a little casket. He wanted to paint it white, but there was no paint in the village either. So he made a paste of flour and water, took some sheets of paper from his daughter's school tablet and pasted them all over the box. From a distance the casket appeared to be painted white.

Meanwhile, the mother and I took the sheet, which Ken and Chris had used when sleeping in the new house, and sewed a little outfit to bury him in. She could not be satisfied unless her baby's body was dressed in white "like an angel," she said. So we made a white gown and tiny white shoes out of poster paper. The mother also wanted poster-paper wings. She believed that if one were not buried in white, he or she could not be an angel, and this was not the time to try to convince her otherwise.

I was concerned about the body decomposing in the heat because it took us so long to get the outfit ready to dress the baby, as the mother kept stopping to cry and talk about Marcos. Finally, eight hours after his death, she was satisfied with the clothes we had made. By now, the stench was almost overwhelming. And when we tried to undress him to bathe him, the little body was so stiff it was hard to remove his clothing. Finally she quit trying and fell in my arms, weeping. "Take the baby, *Hermana.* Bathe him for me."

She watched while I finished the details and laid the beautiful little body in the white casket. At that time an older step-daughter-in-law, who had gathered wild flowers for bouquets, came to attend the funeral. No one else arrived.

While the father went to the cemetery to dig a grave, I decided to stop by our new house, where five of the brothers of the church were working. *"Hermanos,"* I said, "can't you leave your work long enough to accompany the Ramirez family to bury their baby?"

One brother was reluctant. "But they don't go to church," he said, "and we must get this house built for you by tomorrow. It's only a baby, and you know that babies die every day."

But the other men rebuked him. "No, our sister is right. We must show them that Christians care when people have problems." So the five men left the house-building and joined the family as they carried the little white box to the cemetery about a mile out in the jungle.

Marcos died at 8 A.M.; at 5 P.M. that afternoon, we buried him. It was almost dark when I told the family good-bye and walked back to Sapecho, expecting to face another night on the narrow benches in the church, for I was quite certain that there would be no trucks leaving the town until morning.

But there was to be no rest for me that night. When I arrived at the church, a messenger was waiting to direct me to another home where a baby was sick. I walked three miles in the opposite direction to reach the house. By then I was exhausted mentally, emotionally and physically. Seeing another set of beautiful brown eyes clouded with fever and another little stomach rounded from parasites and malnutrition brought me to the brink of despair.

I was neither a nurse nor a doctor. I could not offer any medical help, and there was no other qualified person in the vicinity. All I could do was to pray and to start over again with the same advice: "Please, *Hermana,* take your baby to the doctor."

I knew she would answer, "But, *Hermana,* there is no *mobilidad.*" And I faced again that high, cruel wall of frustration. In my heart, I was sure that Marcos would not have died if we had had a jeep to take him the eighteen kilometers to receive medical care.

◊

That was our welcome to Sapecho. Even before we moved in, we had buried two babies in one week. It seemed too much for me to cope with. I knew it was not God's will for children to suffer like this, but what could we do to help? My mind could not grasp the situation; I felt my brain just shut down, leaving me unable to move, to function, to relate.

I went through the motions of getting food for my family, of smiling and greeting neighbors who passed by my door, but I felt like I was in a deep black hole, in a depression deeper than I could ever have imagined before. How could I go on living…seeing suffering and death like this constantly? We were camping out in our new house to help get it finished. Yet the pot of food I was cooking smelled to me like the little dead bodies as they began to decompose in the tropical heat before we could prepare them for burial.

Our beautiful little church in Sapecho.
A corner of our parsonage is on the left. The foreground is our front yard which we had turned into a garden to grow much-needed food.

I remembered in Kilometer 73 how God had helped me gain the victory over fear for my own children. But now the situation around us seemed so hopeless for everyone, I could not find enough strength even for prayer, except to plead silently, *God, help me! Help the Alto Beni people! Help us all!*

Mr. Barber's Blessing

Very few English-speaking people traveled to Sapecho in those early days, but suddenly we heard the rumble of a *mobilidad*. In the jeep were two retired missionaries whom we had never met before, Mr. and Mrs. Barber, who had stopped by on a last visit to the Alto Beni before returning home. They only lingered an hour or so, but at Ken's invitation, they stayed for lunch, eating the food I could not even bear to smell.

I cannot remember the couple's first names after all these years, but I will never forget what Mr. Barber said to me. After lunch, he called me off to the side of our little house that was still under construction. "Sarah," he began, "you seem overwhelmed with the suffering around you. You know, God is here suffering with these people, too. He loves them more than you do. You don't have to take it all on yourself. That is not God's will for you. He sent you here to help, but you cannot help anyone in this condition. That is all our enemy wants…to keep you from letting God use you here.

"If you want to be part of His work to stop some of this suffering, you have to do what you can, and what you can't do, you must leave in His hands. He sees things from a much bigger perspective. Please let me pray with you that you can give the sorrow to God and start praising Him for sending you here."

While he prayed, I felt the Spirit of God just wrapping us up like the wind softly blowing around us. I had fallen into a trap of caring so much that I could not be useful to God.

I never saw the Barbers again, but when they left, I was an entirely different person. I would continue to hurt just as badly in the future over the great suffering of my neighbors, but God had shown me that if I were to help change things, I had to keep my focus on what He was doing around me and do only my part. A verse of Scripture that I could not have accepted the day before, became real to me and has served me all the years since. "In all things, give thanks, for this is God's will for you in Christ Jesus" (1 Thess. 5:18).

I went to the Sapecho Creek to wash the tears from my face as the Barbers left, and promised God I would stay close behind Him and count on Him to do the things I could not do. Afterward, I visited the homes again where the babies had died. This time, though I wept with the parents, I could also bring the comfort of Jesus as I prayed and thanked God for the lives of the children who had died, for the promise of resurrection and for eternity that we will spend with them.

The grieving families followed my lead and began to thank God for so many little things I had not noticed. His peace filled all our hearts that day.

Home at Last

Shortly after the death of the two babies, the day arrived when our house was finished and ready for us to move to Sapecho. We rented a truck to make the move. When we reached the Beni River, we had to wait an hour for the ferry. When it arrived and we boarded, our truck was so heavy with all our belongings, I thought the ferry might sink, but away we went!

Perched on top of a table sat Tommy, Kiki Dee, as usual, clinging to his hair. Karen was beside him with our pet parrot, Lorito, on her shoulder. The rest of us hung on tightly as we bounced over the narrow, rough road to our new home in the jungle.

Sapecho was a small village with three tiny stores, which sold only a very few items, a school for children from first to the fourth grade, and about two dozen bamboo huts. We knew that a few years later, when the bridge over the Upper Beni River and the new road were slated to be completed, Sapecho would probably be the largest town in the Alto Beni. When we moved in, however, the town was virtually a small community with a handful of bamboo huts.

A few weeks earlier, the church members had offered to help build our house. In one week's time, the three families of the church, with Ken and Chris helping, had completed the job. We provided food and the women cooked over the open fire, as was their custom, to serve the men who were carrying in the materials from the surrounding jungle.

The process was fascinating! First, the men went deep into the jungle to find *mora* trees. From the bark of these trees would come the strong "rope" used for tying seven-inch bamboo posts together to form the corner posts of the house. The men slit the mora bark and peeled it off in long, wide strips, rolled it up, and brought it back to the house site. Here they split the bark into half-inch strips and then peeled off the outer part. While green, the inner strip of bark is tough and pliable.

Next, bamboo canes—two or three inches in diameter—were stuck into the ground to form the walls and tied in place with the strips of inner bark. Then came the tin roof—the main expense of the project—also tied on with mora bark. Not a single nail was used in the construction.

The *hermanos* of the church worked hard and joyfully. It was a beautiful experience to see the men working together, sometimes stopping to sing a hymn or pray a prayer of gratitude when another wall went up. Even the children, as young as three years of age, helped carry the bamboo canes on their little shoulders. As the *hermanos* finished the details, we went back to move our things.

When we drove up in the truck, the workers came out to help transfer our household items the hundred yards from the road to the house. "Come see! Come see!" they urged us. "Your house is big and beautiful!"

The men carried in our one chest of drawers and wardrobe, a double bed for Ken and me and a single bed for each of our four children (many Bolivians sleep on straw mats on the ground), our table and six chairs (many of them do not own a table or chair). Seeing our desk, boxes of books and photographic equipment for developing pictures, they were amazed! Soon the little house, which had seemed so big to them, was full and there was no more room to put anything. They were crushed.

"Oh, *Hermana,*" one of them lamented, "we thought we had made you a big house, but now it looks so small!"

For our part, we thought we had brought only the bare necessities, but their idea of "essentials" and ours were miles apart. Many of the items we had brought were to be used in our ministry to the people—seeds, books, teaching aids, water testing kits, tools, fish nets. Still, it hurt to see their disappointment.

"The house is beautiful," we assured them. "We'll just use a corner of the church next door for our kitchen and another corner for the books. See, as we organize things, it will be fine."

But on Monday morning they were back again, wanting to add a lean-to for a kitchen and a porch. It was a sacrifice for them because some of them had no homestead at all and lived on an urban lot, working for a dollar or two a day in exchange for hard, physical labor. When I realized that they had given up their last week's earnings to help build our house and now wanted to give up more, I swallowed back my tears, receiving a fresh understanding of unselfish giving.

Tommy and Sarah, standing in front of our house after the lean-to for the kitchen and porch was added

Fishing for Minnows

During this phase of the "construction," as we unpacked our boxes, we came to the fish nets. The *hermanos* were thrilled. After eating lunch, they wanted to try the nets. "But where?" Ken asked. "The river is several kilometers away."

"In our little Sapecho stream," they replied with enthusiasm.

"But that stream is only about ankle-deep in most places," Ken pointed out. "You mean you have fish big enough to eat?" They assured him that there were many.

We followed and watched as the men eagerly scooped up the fish—actually minnows, only about an inch or an inch and a half long—in the nets. They caught a bowl full and returned to work, talking about the fish dinner we would enjoy that night. Since protein is so difficult to obtain in Sapecho, this would be a rare treat indeed. In spite of that, I did not share their anticipation of our supper of minnows.

When the day's work was done, however, I joined them, squatting on the ground around the bowl of fried, whole minnows. They prayed a sincere prayer of thanks for the fish net and the fish, and then each of them reached into the bowl with their fingers for their share of minnows.

I held my breath, looking around for Tommy. He had not appreciated the fact that we were coming to Bolivia and since arriving, he, more than the other children, had been critical of the food and the customs. I just knew he wouldn't eat those minnows—eyes, tail, and all! Further, I was afraid he might offend them by not eating.

But, no…there he was in the circle with the rest, his monkey still clinging to his hair. As I watched, he reached into the bowl, took out a handful of minnows, chewed them up and handed one up to his monkey. I quit worrying about Tommy then and realized that he was adjusting to Bolivia just fine, after all.

We moved our kitchen into the lean-to addition, although the roof was not yet finished. We had decided to use the rest of the money designated for the house to buy chicken wire for a fence to keep the neighbor's pigs, sheep, dogs, chickens and babies out of the garden we wanted to plant. Instead of tin roofing, we now must use thatch, made out of palm leaves.

Hermano Fermin, one of our church members, an Aymaran man, was a master in the art of using palm leaves. He carefully directed the gathering of the long leaves. Then they were split in half. When tied onto the roof, the first layer used the left side of the leaves; the second layer, the right side of the leaves. Each stem was tied above the other with the *mora* bark. It was truly a work of art.

Rain, Rain, Go Away!

While we were in the middle of the roofing job, the rainy season started. For two weeks it rained almost incessantly—hard, driving downpours. The water flooded our house, blowing in the open windows and through the bamboo sides. It filled the kitchen, where the roof was only half-finished. There was not a dry spot in the house! All the beds were damp. Our clothes were all wet. The dirt floor was now ankle-deep in mud, and a puddle of water ran three feet across the middle of the room.

Cooking became a skating competition to see who could slip and slide from the stove to the table without falling. In addition to the weather conditions, all the neighbors crowded into our house to pass the long rainy days. They went through all our boxes and drawers, asking endless questions about the contents. They were good people; they wouldn't steal. They were only curious about the strange new items they found—medicines, kits to test water, etc. And it was a good time for us to get to know the people we had come to serve.

When the rain finally ended, I walked down the trail through the jungle growth to the home of our next-door neighbor, *Hermano* Fermin, where his wife was cooking supper. "What are you having tonight?" I asked, just to make conversation.

"Soup," she replied.

I could see their one pot filled with water, heating over the open fire. There was one small diced onion, a clove of garlic, and the spice they use to flavor everything, cumin. This was not soup, but flavored water! Suddenly, I knew that this meager meal was all they had because they had forfeited their last week's wages to spend their time in building our house.

Most touching of all was the thought that these people did not consider any of this a "sacrifice." Over and over they welcomed us and thanked us for coming. Fourteen years before our arrival, the first homesteaders had founded the village of Sapecho. "But you are the first religious leaders who have ever lived in Sapecho *with* us," they said. "We have prayed so long for a pastor to teach us the Word of God. And now God has answered our prayers."

With us. The words rang in my heart. Yes, this was our covenant with the Bolivian church and with these people—to be *with them* for two years. I thought of Christ—the Son of the Living God—

coming to earth to dwell *with us* here. Immanuel—
"God with us." The ministry of His Presence.
Could we do any less?

Chapter Five

The Jungle in Our House
by Ken Corson

How many are your works, O LORD!
In wisdom You made them all;
the earth is full of Your creatures.
—Psalm 104:24

After the rain stopped and the thatched roof was finished, the mud floor dried out and we settled in. Inside, our house was a dirt floor and nothing else. No closets or room dividers—just one open room and a lean-to for a kitchen. Only "walls" made of bamboo separated the inside from the outside. The "windows" were open spaces in the bamboo. Vampire bats and mosquitoes flew freely through our house at night, and other small creatures had no difficulty getting in.

There was no electricity in the whole town. We had no refrigeration, television, telephone, bathroom or other civilized amenities. Friends back home would have sent us money to buy some of these things, but we had agreed—and were determined to keep our word—to live on the level of our neighbors.

Some of our friends could not understand our decision to live as our neighbors lived, but I must sincerely say that it was the greatest learning experience of our lives. It also helped us understand others in the community and taught us an important principle of development: Decisions about how the community develops must be made by the people who will live with the results of the development scheme, not by others who have not lived in their cultural context.

So many well-meaning people came to visit, wanting to give us things that were not really appropriate for our needs. But when visitors asked what we needed—and most of them did—we had an opportunity to explain. We soon learned that one must spend time in a culture to understand what is important and what is not.

When we began to set up housekeeping, we hung the mosquito nets as we had been taught to do. We had to bring all water in buckets from the creek and then boil it over an open fire for fifteen minutes to purify it. We had to build an outhouse. We needed everything at once…and everything took time. We were stressed to find the time to collect food and cook over an open fire, wash clothes by hand, and teach our children's school lessons. Much of our time was spent attending to our neighbors' emergencies. Sickness was rampant.

Every night, we would go to bed exhausted, often not having even begun what we had planned to do that day. Even on our small Bolivian salary, time was more scarce than money; it took so much time just to survive. We were shocked by how long it took us to accomplish our tasks. We estimated that it took a month in the jungle to do what would only have taken three days back home. However, because of the lack of electricity, we could not do much work after dark, so we had to relax in the evenings. And in the midst of the stress of the daily rush, we had wonderful times of fellowship with our own children and with our neighbors. There were so many new things to learn, and everyday was an adventure, even though the pace did not let up.

When the Sun Goes Down

When the sun goes down in the jungle, it gets very dark. Inside, however, *mecheros* were our main form of illumination. *Mecheros* were beer cans filled with kerosene with a twisted rag to serve as a wick. Flashlights were used sparingly because there were no batteries available in Sapecho.

With one *mechero* burning, we would get in bed, a process that required keeping our feet off the floor so we would not bring dirt in with us. The legs of each bed sat in small tuna fish cans of water to keep the ants and other unwelcome critters from climbing in. We had to be careful also to fasten the mosquito net at the bottom so it would not furnish a ladder for creepy-crawlies. Needless to say, we could not simply "hop into bed."

Since we were all in the same room, we could lie there and talk to each other. Every night each member of our family shared experiences of the day. Often, we would have been engaged in different tasks, and this was the time to tell the others what had happened.

No day was a dud. Every single one was filled with adventure, interesting happenings and experiences. Everything was so different, so unfamiliar, so new. None of us was ever bored, even though witnessing the suffering of the sick distressed all of us.

Chris would pull his guitar under the mosquito net in his bed and serenade us at night. Sometimes we joined in. Hymns and gospel songs were a normal part of our evenings before we nodded off to sleep. Chris also included John Denver and The Eagles in his repertoire. To this day, the guitar instrumental "Malageña" and the song "Sunshine on my Shoulder" remind me of those special, good days our family shared in our little jungle home. Chris would blow out the *mechero* when he stepped outside his mosquito net to hang up his guitar for the evening.

In the peak of our thatched roof, millions of mosquitoes hummed more music as we drifted off to sleep. Under our nets, the bugs could not reach us. On dark nights the bats flew through our house, feasting on the mosquitoes, but they stayed away from our netting. Fatigue from physical activity, stars sparkling from our last glimpses of the evening, echoes of music and the memories of the day were more pleasant to our tired minds than anything Hollywood could have provided.

Without television, telephones, movies and shopping malls, the children discovered a real world with real people, many of them struggling to survive. They learned that even though they were young, their contribution would make a big difference in this world.

Instead of a classroom, our children had a jungle, a new culture, another language and more experiences than some people have all their life long. Part of their real world included animals that replaced manufactured distractions. The black-draped darkness and the sound stage of the jungle were dramatic backdrops for some of our exotic family pets.

KiKi Dee, Rodeo-Rider

Kiki Dee, our pet monkey, came to us when a neighbor killed the monkey's mother for food. Though Tommy claimed the baby monkey, the whole family enjoyed him. Kiki spent a large part of the day hanging onto Tommy's hair, riding on his head wherever our son went. It was more rewarding than wearing a coonskin cap. Need I mention that Tom had to wash his hair in the creek numerous times during the day?

Karen, with Kiki Dee

We put a cloth belt around Kiki's tiny waist to keep him from running off, but he was quite an escape artist. Once, he scurried to the top of the thatched roof, holding a spider half his size. Kiki would pull off a leg at a time and chew on it as a human being would chew on a piece of Kentucky Fried Chicken.

Hermano Mauricio, our next-door neighbor and the grandfather in our church, had recently brought a sheep down from the Andes. We learned that sheep and llamas needed the cool weather of the mountains and did not fare well in the heat of Sapecho. One day, as Tommy ran down the trail between our houses with Kiki on his head, they suddenly encountered the neighbor's sheep, which was grazing nearby. With no warning, Kiki jumped from Tommy's head and landed on the woolly back of *Hermano* Mauricio's prized sheep. This startled the animal. He bolted and ran for his life, with Kiki mounted on his back like a cowboy in a rodeo.

Hermano Mauricio wrung his hands in desperation. "My poor sheep with his coat of wool will run himself to death if someone doesn't stop him!" Chris and Tommy ran after him, but the frightened sheep continued to run around and around the entire village with Kiki Dee astride. All the other boys along the way joined in the chase, and to our great relief, the group managed to corner the sheep and hold him until Tommy could grab the delinquent Kiki and take him home.

Kiki was not the only animal in the family.

At different times we had a parrot, a three-toed sloth, a pair of baby ocelots and a wounded hawk. Our children were not deprived by living where nature and simple things were a stage for us to live out some of our most meaningful and memorable days. We did not need a barrel of monkeys. One, named Kiki Dee, was enough for our family.

The Day the Whole House Shook

Everyone in the community came to know that our children loved animals. On numerous occasions, we had a menagerie of critters. One of the strangest of these was a three-toed sloth. In the Alto Beni, these were called *peresozos*, which means "lazy" in Spanish.

A sloth's movements are deliberate, as if moving in slow motion. Folklore says that if they get their arms around something or someone, they will not let go; one would have to cut the arms off! We never had to experience that, so I can't say if this is fact or fiction, but these people certainly believe it.

This was a weird-looking creature. Its tiny chin receded into its neck and the top of its head was nearly round. The whole body, including the head, was covered with a densely matted fur. The eyes were glassy and did not look intelligent, but presented an image that would have been at home with Frankenstein. Its mouth was frozen in a constant smile, as if pretending to be innocent while contemplating a mischievous joke it was about to play on someone. Its three toes contained long, menacing nails, which were used to tear off the bark of a tree or dig into a mound or nest to retrieve sustenance. The children made a rope of some old rags, tied the sloth around its middle and used the rope as a leash.

That night there was no moon. Tommy had tied the sloth outside to the bamboo post at the corner of our house, leaving the animal four or five feet of leash. Suddenly, when we were all sleeping, a sense of movement jolted me awake. I sat up in bed, still groggy with sleep, and heard the whir of wings as a bat flew by our mosquito net. But that was commonplace here. No, the bat had not awakened me.

I reached under my pillow for a flashlight. Shining it across our room, I could see that the mosquito nets on all our beds were moving, dancing up and down like marionettes. Then I saw the thatched roof above us, slightly swaying back and forth. There was no wind, so what could be causing that? Was our house about to collapse? I quickly put on my sandals and slid out of bed without waking anyone.

Stepping outside, I saw that the sloth had managed to climb up the corner post of our house until he came to the end of the leash. Instead of stopping or giving up, the sloth continued to stretch, determined to climb higher. His arms were so strong, he was jerking the whole house. When I shone the light on the post, it fell upon a sinister-looking smile, the lighting exaggerating the grotesque features that were bad enough in the daytime.

Since it was the middle of the night, I wanted to get back to sleep. I untied the cloth rope and let the sloth climb a nearby tree, not bothering to re-tie the rope. After all, this thing was so slow, it couldn't go very far…or so I thought. The next morning the creature was gone. We only had the sloth one day. I could not help feeling relieved.

Fever Ants under the Bed

One day some new friends came to our house to visit our twelve-year-old Kathy. As the girls sat on her bed looking through some of her pictures, one of her friends suddenly pointed to the floor under Kathy's bed. "Buna!" she said excitedly.

The Alto Beni region has a large ant, an inch or an inch and a half long, which the local people call a buna, or fever ant. The bite is very painful and leaves its victim with a fever for more than twenty-four hours.

We all came running and got on our knees to watch this hole in the ground under Kathy's bed with many bunas crawling in and out. Their trail led through the bamboo wall to the outside of the house. This was a dangerous insect to have living right under her bed.

"Those are the same ants I saw last night, crawling over my mosquito net!" Kathy gasped. "I didn't know they were bunas! I was reading in bed by the light of the *mechera*, and shadows started walking across the page of my book. I looked up, and there was a line of ants marching across my mosquito net, right over my head! I would have screamed for help if I had know they were bunas. I thought they were just ordinary ants and couldn't get inside my net, so I kept reading until I fell asleep. Imagine! Bunas under me and over me!"

Discovering the threat was one thing. Now, what were we to do about it? We had no pest control company to call nor a phone to call on. We had no pesticides and no store to buy any.

One of our neighbors, hearing of our buna nest, offered to help. I was curious as to how he planned to handle this problem. I was certain that Kathy would not sleep in her bed with bunas under it.

Our neighbor came into the house, carrying his machete. I was surprised. I had never thought of fighting ants with a machete. He brought a strong stick in also. He sat down on the dirt floor and waited. Before long, a buna crawled out of the hole. The man put his machete in its path, and the buna continued to crawl up on the flat side. Then the man used the stick to squash the ant. One by one, other bunas met the same fate. For several hours, our dear neighbor, with infinite patience, dispatched a great many fever ants in this way.

My logical mind was thinking, *This is ridiculous!* Deep in the ground was a nest with a queen. Killing bunas one at a time wasn't going to put an end to all of them.

But my neighbor was ahead of me. I watched as he made up some kind of liquid concoction. I think he mixed the squashed ants with water, but I never did know for sure. Then he dug out a hollow in the entrance to their nest with the tip of his machete and poured this mixture into the hole.

Kathy slept with her sister Karen that night. After keeping an eye on the buna highway for two days, we saw no more bunas. Kathy returned to her bed, glad that the fever ants were gone.

Tommy and Lorito, the parrot

Lorito, Our Little Parrot

Indoor animals tend to be treated as family members. When a neighbor gave us a parrot,

Lorito became part of the family. All of us tried to get Lorito to talk. "Polly want a cracker?" we would coax him, all to no avail. Other words and bribes were attempted, but this bird was mute.

Despite this failure, Lorito was accepted by the rest of our menagerie. We had a pet *tejon*, which looked like a cross between a raccoon and an anteater. Then there were Kiki Dee and Tommy's dog, Johnny Reb. Outside was Porky, the pig. And, of course, chickens and ducks.

One day I took the children with me, leaving Sarah alone to have some quiet time at home. As she was writing letters on our table, she was surprised to hear one of the children call her loudly, "Momma!" She got up to see which child had come back unexpectedly, but there was no one in the house or yard. She was mystified, but decided she had imagined hearing "Momma!" as the children called when they discovered something new or exciting to share.

But then one of them called her again, very clearly and distinctly, "Momma!" This time she searched more earnestly, but with the same results: no children were to be found. Just then she heard the peeping of baby chicks inside the house. How had that mother hen and her chicks gotten in again?! She rushed around the bed toward the sound, but there were no chicks in sight. She thought that she was losing her mind.

Suddenly, right over her head, from the rafters, came the call again, "Momma!" followed by the sound of chicks peeping. She looked up to find Lorito continuing his ventriloquist act, using the very same intonation as our children. Instead of reading readiness, this must have been talking readiness that developed all at once. She was very relieved to know she wasn't imagining things!

Lorito's great vice was eating soap. In the context of our jungle living with so few luxuries, hand soap was not something to waste. We were able to keep soap, but we had to get it when we traveled to La Paz, almost two hundred miles away, and we didn't make the long trip often. After discovering Lorito's strange penchant, we had to keep our soap supply protected from our feathered predator. But the bird entertained us enough to repay our vigilance.

Our Bald-Headed Tejon

One day a neighbor brought Tommy an unfamiliar animal. They called it a tejon; it evidently was related to the raccoon because it looked similar and had a tail with ringed patterns, although its nose looked more like an anteater. Tommy found its picture in *World Book* and discovered that its English name was "coatimundi." Like a kitten, it loved to curl up and go to sleep in our laps. But what curiosity it had! It had to explore everything!

From his last trip to La Paz, Chris had brought us a can of jelly, a rare treat in the Alto Beni. We did not even have a can opener since there were so few cans of food here. We were able to open the can with our Swiss army knife, but we didn't bother to cut the lid all the way off. After eating the contents, we threw the empty can into the trash basket.

There was, however, a residue of jelly stuck to the can and to the inside of the lid. Tejon discovered this little delicacy and stuck his snout into the can. While his snout and mouth were inside the can, the jelly stuck to the fur on his head.

Before daylight, ants had found the jelly on Tejon's head and devoured his hair along with the jelly. We were shocked the next morning at the appearance of our bald-headed Tejon. It was quite a spectacle!

Can you picture our little one-room home? The floor was Tejon's domain. Lorito, the parrot, had a perch about eye level and often sat on the window opening, calling out to us. Kiki Dee, when he wasn't on Tommy's head, was bouncing on the tops of our mosquito nets, jumping from one bed to the other on his self-discovered trampolines.

Tiger in the House!

A small boy came up to our window one day and stood there, his eyes wide. Finally, glancing back down the trail, he spoke up somewhat timidly, *"Hermana,* they are coming with tigers!"

I followed his gaze and saw two of the homesteaders surrounded by a group of children. In each of the homesteader's arms was a baby wildcat, meowing loudly.

I understood from our geography books that there were no real tigers in South America, but there were many kinds of large wildcats, which the local people called "tigers." According to a book with pictures of the wild in this area, we felt sure these little fellows were ocelots.

"My dog led me to the nest, but the mother cat got away," the first homesteader explained. "What a shame we lost her. If I had only had a rifle! These tigers are a plague. They kill our farm animals. And this one is still on the prowl right on my farm. But at least I got her babies."

I took one of the little ones in my arms, amazed at his beautiful soft fur. He was more cuddly than a kitten. "They make good pets if you train them," the other man broke in. "Would you like to buy them?"

That was all our children wanted to hear. Did they ever want two baby tigers! But the kittens were so young, their eyes were barely open. Someone would have to feed them all through the day and wake up to feed them in the night too. And what would we give them to eat when they grew up? Very little meat was available here for human beings, much less for animals.

We would have been swamped with pets had some of the ones the children brought home not escaped—like the armadillo Tommy had his eye on. Now the monkey was well-trained, but the new baby coatimundo was a real mischief-maker. "No!" I said emphatically. "We absolutely cannot buy two tigers!"

John and Rachelle hold the baby ocelots.

At this time John and Rachelle Stevenson from Alabama were volunteering to help us for several weeks. Rachelle wanted the ocelets as much as our children did. The homesteader clearly had no interest in keeping them; he wanted to sell them. "Keep them a week or so," he offered, "and see if they live. Then you can decide."

The children and Rachelle immediately began to fix them a bed in a box. Rachelle really wanted to sleep with them, but John objected. We were late with supper because of the excitement of the *tigrecillos*, as the people here called them. We ate by candlelight, left the dishes till morning, fed the baby ocelots and went to bed.

It was one o'clock in the morning when we heard Rachelle urgently calling from their makeshift bedroom in the corner of the church next door. In one moment I was wide awake. It sounded like a thousand dogs were fighting in our yard. But there was one deep snarl amidst the uproar that could not have come from a dog.

Grabbing our shoes and a flashlight, we rushed out in time to see the dogs disappearing down the trail. I think every dog in Sapecho was in the fracas.

"It was the mother tiger!" Rachelle screamed. "She's taken the kittens!" Later, we wished she had, but the dogs had stopped her before she could get to them. When all quieted down, we went back to bed, but John and Rachelle could not sleep.

"She'll come back!" John insisted. "I know she'll come back!"

They lay down on their bed in a corner of the church——John, with a flashlight in one hand, a knife in the other. There was no way to close the open spaces in the church wall that served as windows, but they hoped the dogs would warn them if she returned.

The mother ocelot was smart. An hour later

she returned from the opposite direction, coming in from the jungle behind our house. No dog picked up her scent this time. Suddenly, Rachelle and John heard her jump up on the bamboo cane along the open windows. She walked across the cords that held up their pup tent, which they used over their bed as a mosquito net. The tent began to shake. They froze. Would she attack? Her two babies were in a box nearby. How glad Rachelle was that they were not in bed with them!

Rachelle and John hardly breathed as the big cat stalked across the window ledge above their bed. Then with a bound, she was on the ground at their feet, nosing around the box. The babies awoke and meowed; the mother answered with a warning growl and immediately they hushed. She pushed the top of the box part-way open, stuck her head in and sniffed them. She waited awhile at the foot of their bed, then jumped back up on the high window ledge and disappeared.

She was gone. A South American tiger, or more properly, a full-grown ocelot, had actually been in the church which served as Rachelle and John's home away from home, and walked right over them. They drew in a deep sigh of relief.

Why didn't she take the little ones? Some

of our neighbors say she renounced them because they had a strong human smell by now. Others expected her to come back at any moment. Still others said she never really came…that it was only a nightmare—a tiger would never enter someone's house even to retrieve her young. But John and Rachelle knew differently.

We all wished we could give the babies back to her, but the neighbors would be furious, because the little wildcats would grow up to kill their chickens. Rachelle considered taking them back to Alabama with her, but found that the authorities would not permit it. We definitely did not want the *tigrecillos*, but couldn't decide what to do.

We kept the babies for several months, until suddenly one day, they were missing. We never knew what happened to them, but we imagined that one of the local homesteaders had solved the problem for us by getting rid of them when we were not at home. It was a relief in a way, but it made us sad to think of killing the beautiful creatures, although we knew some animals really need to stay in their own habitats.

We continued to be amazed at the different kinds of animals that surrounded us in the tropics. As the children filled our little house with them, it was almost like we were bringing the jungle inside. The more we learned of the rain forest, the more we felt like praising God for His wonderful works of creation. Psalm 104 became a hymn of praise for us, especially verse 24: "How many are your works, O LORD! In wisdom You made them all. The earth is full of Your creatures!"

(opposite page)
Chris, (right) with a group of *hermanos* in a dugout canoe, going down the Big River to another village that had asked us to bring them the Word of God.

Chapter Six

Sickness in the Rainy Season

On a steamy Sunday in early spring, Kathy, Tommy and I started to a worship service on the other side of the Beni River, leaving Karen with Ken who would be leading the Sapecho services.

Chris had crossed the river the night before to get some supplies and spend the night with the Caufields.

The river was up that day, running very swiftly, and the motor on the ferry burned out as we started across. The runaway ferry crashed through some canoes tied up at the bank, knocked a man into the river and plunged downstream at a rapid rate. We caught a glimpse of the man our boat had run over, coming up from the water on the other side and pulling himself onto the bank as we were washed around the bend.

The Upper Beni is a large river, and on this day it was at flood stage; it whipped that ferry around as though it were a leaf in the stream. There were only four passengers—Tommy, Kathy, a soldier with a puppy and I, along with Jaime, our friend who ran the ferry. Jaime was desperately trying to steer the boat to shore, but in vain. As a skilled boatman, he knew the river currents. He knew, too, that a little farther down, the Suapi River emptied into the Beni, which would make it even harder to stop. Below that were the rapids. "Hang on!" Jaime yelled to us. "Hold on tight!"

Then we saw them coming. Some of the indigenous men who had rigged outboard motors on their dug-out canoes came flying down that river. How dignified they looked as they stood straight and tall in their canoes, skimming over the water at top speed. Like lightning they passed us, and after gaining some distance below, they slowed and turned back. Coming from downstream, they ran into the ferry, trying to stop us. Three, then four canoes rushed into us, but the ferry just pushed them along, even though their motors were straining at top power. Five canoes, then six. Only then were they able to halt our race toward destruction. Although they could do nothing to push us back upstream, the canoes held the ferry steady in the raging current.

Jaime yelled to us to jump into one of the canoes. All four of us hurried to follow his instruction, but Tommy turned back to pick up the puppy the soldier had forgotten. Leaping into the canoe with the dog, he sat down in the center with the rest of us, much to my relief.

"Mama, are we going to end up in the Amazon?" Kathy asked shakily.

"No, we'll never make it past the rapids!" Tommy called back. "If the canoe turns over, head for that bank...it's nearer," he warned his sister. "And be ready to swim hard!"

The seventh canoe zipped by, turned and came back to add its powerful thrust. One boatman, who seemed to know the currents better than the others, yelled out above the roar of the water, directing them all toward one side. Slowly, inch by inch, we began making our way up the river. About half an hour later, we were back where we started, and the boatman took us on across the river in his canoe.

Glad to have our feet on solid ground, even if it was muddy, we hurried on past the Caufields, where Chris joined us, to cross the smaller Suapi River where a man waited for customers in a balsa boat. The rafts made of balsa logs were very light. They would go underwater a few inches when one stepped on them, but they wouldn't sink all the way. A cable spanned the Suapi overhead; the raft was connected to the cable so that it wouldn't be washed downstream while the boatman poled us across. We did get our feet wet, but we made it fine.

After climbing the steep mountain on the other side of the river, we arrived at the house where the service was to be held. Waiting for us were some thirty people—a good crowd for such a sparsely settled rural community. Since we arrived at noon, the homeowners who were hosting the service were already serving lunch. They had roasted a whole pig for the occasion. Afterward, the people sang and we shared. Others gave their testimonies, and they all sang some more.

Chris became concerned that it was going to be dark before we could get back to the Big River, and he might not be able to make the crossing. His dad needed the supplies that Chris had bought, so by the middle of the afternoon, he excused himself and went ahead. It would have been impolite for me to leave early, but we knew Kathy, Tommy and I could spend the night at the Caufields if it were too late to go on to Sapecho.

Around 4 P.M. we concluded the service and dismissed the people. After saying our goodbyes, we slipped and slid down the steep mountain trail until we arrived at the Suapi. The owner of the balsa raft was waiting to take us across for a quarter. When I apologized for causing him to wait so long, he assured me that he had not waited. He had gone to his home nearby, where he could hear some of the service, and planned to return when the singing ended.

"Then you were not here to take our son across the river earlier?" I asked him.

"No, I wasn't expecting anyone until the

service was over," he explained. "But as I was coming out of my house, I saw a young man pulling himself across the cable, hand over hand. I guess he got tired about halfway, because he stopped and slung his legs up over the cable and hung—head down—for a minute to rest his hands. I'm sorry for what happened after that…"

"What *did* happen?" I asked, my heart pounding.

"Well, all of a sudden, the kid fell into the river headfirst. He was washed down before I could get to the bank to help him. He swam hard, but he made it, and I saw him climb out way down at the bend," the boatman explained. "Like I said, I'm just sorry I wasn't here to take him across."

We had to suppose that Chris was all right, since the boatman did say he had seen him climb out of the river. But we were so concerned to know how our son was, we didn't even stop at the Caufields. We rushed on as fast as we could walk to Puerto Linares to take the ferry. Of course, it was not running this evening, as the motor had blown out earlier, but we did get a man with a canoe to risk taking us across the swollen stream. We made it and even caught the *Servicio Rapido* for a ride home.

How happy we were to see Chris already there. I was beginning to sympathize with him because of his fall from the cable, but he laughed. "I didn't fall at all!" he declared. "I dived in on purpose. My wallet fell out of my pocket and was floating down the river. It had my American motorcycle license in it...so there was no way I was going to let that get away!"

In Bolivia you have to be twenty-one to get a license to drive, but here, because the police didn't read English, they would look at Chris's motorcycle license and assume it was a license to drive a car. Even though we had no vehicle, he didn't want to lose that license in case he ever needed it. With a big grin on his face, our fifteen-year old pulled a soaked motorcycle license out of his pocket!

Sick with Fever

The rainy season continued in the Alto Beni with a vengeance, as if trying to make up for its late arrival. The Beni River was over its banks, and all adjoining areas were flooded.

There was a big puddle of water in the middle of our floor again. Sick with a fever, I preferred my bed over trying to cross the raging river to reach a doctor.

Lying there in our little water-logged hut, the frightening experience of fighting the river the Sunday before was still fresh in my mind. I kept hoping to feel better without having to call for outside help.

We knew that God had the power to heal. We had witnessed His healing power many times… sometimes directly and sometimes through doctors. I had often reflected on the verse in Matthew 4:23: "Jesus went throughout Galilee, teaching in their synagogues, preaching the good news of the kingdom, and healing every disease and sickness among the people."

As true followers of Jesus, we had gone throughout the Alto Beni, preaching the "good news of the kingdom." But, oh, how we wanted to heal the sick among the people too! Sometimes God used our prayers and our little bottle of Pepto Bismol to save children from dehydration and to give them a chance to live longer. But at other times, it was not enough, and they died. It took awhile, but we had learned to trust God with the bigger picture that we could not see.

Now it was my own body that needed healing. I felt desperately sick. I did not know whether God was going to heal me, but I knew I could trust Him to do whatever was best. After two or three days, when it appeared that I was getting worse, we knew that we must seek medical help. As was true so often in the past, there was no *mobilidad.*

◊

Finally, after nearly a week, we heard a vehicle coming. Ken picked me up and carried me out to the road, covering me from the constant rain with a piece of plastic. On our way to the clinic in Kilometer 73, we caught a ride on a truck that took us as far as the river. But the river was too high for the ferry to cross.

Instead, we crossed by canoe-taxi and then started the two-mile walk to Kilometer 73. I was too sick and weak to walk more than a few steps at a time. Even with my family's help, I had to pray for God's strength each step of the way.

Suddenly we saw the jeep approaching. It was Rosa Caufield, coming into town to buy food for the high school. She saw us, stopped, turned around and took us to the doctor. How thankful we were for a *mobilidad!*

For the next few days, I was treated in

the little hospital at Kilometer 73. The medical personnel suggested to Ken that I needed more care than they could offer and that he should try to get me to the capital city, La Paz.

With only a few seats available on the bus, Ken knew that he could not take all six of us. Since he could not leave the younger children, Chris and Kathy went with me on the bus back up that long muddy road. After eleven days of illness, I arrived at the Methodist Hospital in La Paz and was quickly diagnosed with hepatitis.

A Grand Reunion

The day after Chris and Kathy accompanied me into the Andean high country and admitted me to the hospital, Chris woke up with typhoid fever and was admitted to the same hospital. After that, our Kathy spent her time running from one room to the other to take care of us both.

Ken, in the meantime, managed to get transportation out of Sapecho and came to La Paz with the other two children to see about us. Of course, there were no phones to let us know they were coming, so we were surprised and overjoyed when they arrived so unexpectedly.

Ken was eager to share all the news from Sapecho. "The good news is that we finished the outhouse, a pig pen and the chicken house." His demeanor changed slightly. "The bad news is that we've run out of chicken wire. We did string up enough to keep out the dogs and sheep and pigs, not to mention the constant stream of little children, poking into all our drawers and boxes." He grinned. "I guess that's a start."

I agreed. These were the essentials. If we could cultivate a garden and raise some chickens and pigs, we could have a balanced diet. So far, we had existed mostly on rice, yucca, macaroni and bananas.

Ken looked tired. I noticed that he had lost more weight and his eyes were bloodshot. I insisted that he get an examination while he was here, but he only laughed. "I'm fine," he said. "Now, you're better, and as soon as Chris improves, we'll be going back to Sapecho."

He had a lot more to tell me. "The young men of the community—about eight of them, all in their twenties—have been coming to help me with my work and to talk," Ken went on. "They've asked me to help them start a youth group and some classes for adults who can't read. There are so many of them in the community, you know. And these boys want to start a library in the church, for there are almost no books available."

In his enthusiasm, he got up and began to pace. "The leaders of the community have also asked me to help them with a water project to get safe drinking water for the town—like the Caufields did for Kilometer 73. Of course, we know that the contaminated water is the cause of so much death and disease around here. I went with them and we made a survey of the springs and water sources available."

On and on Ken talked, encouraged by the response of the people in Sapecho and the opportunity for really doing something to help there. "Our fish project has stirred up a lot of interest too," he continued. "Homesteaders have come from miles around, wanting to be part of it. And we have set up a meeting for the Heifer Project representatives to meet the Sapecho homesteaders. They've promised to try to get a heifer for each farmer. The farmers will reimburse them by returning the first calf. The men are excited about the possibility of getting their own cow—only two of them have one now.

"Then the church is planning to invite the

whole district to a retreat in May; that means we'll have to build more benches and an altar and pulpit before then…." His voice trailed off and he sat back down, obviously fatigued.

"It all sounds great, Ken. But look at you! You're exhausted, and I don't like your color. Will you promise me that you'll get a checkup so you won't get sick like Chris and me?"

He shook his head and waved off my concern. "Oh, it's just the altitude. Tomorrow, while I'm still here in La Paz, I have to stop by some government offices. There's a possibility I can get the road service equipment to make our first fish pond, since it's a non-profit, community project. If not, digging the pond by hand will delay us by several months."

◊

But when tomorrow came, Ken could not stand up. When he was diagnosed with another form of typhoid, he was immediately assigned to the same room as Chris.

Poor Kathy had her hands full, waiting on all three of us. In Latin America, it is often customary for a member of the family to stay with those hospitalized at all times. But I felt sorry for Kathy, who celebrated her thirteenth birthday while waiting on her sick mother, father and brother. How long she had waited for this day…and now it would be spent in a strange city, thousands of miles from her friends in America.

We were all surprised when, that very afternoon, two of the pastors' wives from the area came to the hospital with a birthday cake for Kathy! They had graciously taken note of our birthdays in their church records. Knowing that North Americans often celebrate birthdays with a cake, and yet with no ovens to bake in, they had bought the cake at a bakery. It was a small pound cake with no icing, but it meant everything to Kathy.

Meanwhile, we had to leave Tommy and Karen at the Methodist Center, which offered beds for travelers. La Paz was a big, strange city, and the children didn't begin to know where to look for food, but the kind people in the city's churches heard that we were sick. They did not let Karen and Tommy miss a meal.

Our brothers and sisters in Christ took turns bringing them food or taking the children into their homes. Even though they were strangers, Tommy and Karen felt that they had a big family taking care of them. And Kathy will never forget her thirteenth birthday and how those *hermanas* celebrated with her in the hospital during a time of serious family illness. That incident was an important step in helping Kathy and our other children feel that Bolivia was truly home.

Homecoming

When Ken and Chris were dismissed from the hospital, they headed back down to Sapecho with Tommy and Karen. A local pastor's family took me in so I could recuperate near the doctor. Kathy stayed in La Paz to care for me.

After another month, the doctor declared that I was roadworthy. I almost felt like someone returning from near death, stepping out into a new life, as we boarded the bus to leave La Paz early that morning. It had been a long month of recovery, but now I felt well.

All day we traveled down the narrow mountain ledge of a road, but now we had become more used to it, and it didn't frighten us as it had the first time. In Caranavi, some five hours from our destination, the bus line stopped, and we began to look for a truck to take us the rest of the way. At dark, we found one, but the driver said he would not be leaving until 3 A.M. the next morning.

We spent the night sleeping on the church floor, thankful for a roof over our heads. True to his word, the driver blew his horn for us at 3 A.M. sharp. By 7 A.M. we were at the ferry in Puerto Linares, ready to cross, but the ferry motor was out of order again. We waited six hours, so eager to get to Sapecho, only sixteen kilometers on the other side of that river. Unaware of our desire to get home, the river, which had returned to its normal size, flowed peacefully along, halting our progress. By late afternoon, the motor was finally repaired and we were on our way again.

As we entered Sapecho, the driver announced our arrival with a blast of his horn. Ken, the children and the neighbors dropped their work and hurried to the road to greet us. They had been working in the hot sun and their faces were sweaty and streaked with dirt, but never had they looked so beautiful to me!

Even our little hut was transformed. I immediately took note of the new kitchen sink. Outside the kitchen, Ken had also built an elevated platform that held a 55-gallon barrel. When he and the boys filled the barrel with buckets of water from the Sapecho stream, we now had running water, thanks to gravity and a length of pipe.

Other welcome additions were the outdoor latrine and some more privacy walls, created by sewing straw mats to bamboo frames. Outside were the newly planted garden and the chicken wire fence to keep out the neighbors' livestock. Not only that—but we were now the proud owners of a pig and a pen, along with five young chickens, which Chris had bought in Kilometer 73.

And then—another surprise—the one hen we had before was setting on ten eggs! This gave us hope for more protein in our diet. I ignored the fact that the hen was setting in the box of Karen's clothes at the foot of her bed. Karen was content to rotate the few clothes she had that were outside the box so as not to disturb the hen.

The road service had loaned Ken a bulldozer to help with the fish project, and eight urban lots behind us, which had grown up in jungle, were cleared. Already, one of the fish-breeding ponds was almost dug. How wonderful everything looked to me. How hard Ken and the children had labored to get so much done. More than a month had passed during my illness. Now that month was over and almost forgotten in the joy of being back home in Sapecho.

When we went to bed, I thought I heard bees swarming, but Ken assured me it was only mosquitoes. As the rainy season had progressed, the mosquitoes had increased. Safe under our netting, we nodded off to a symphony of humming wings making music all around us.

Midnight Crisis

We hadn't slept long before we were awakened by a neighbor's urgent call. "Come, *hermanos!* A brother has come for help. His wife is dying!"

Grabbing our shoes, we ran down the trail behind her. We entered a one-room hut, which was more than half-filled with rice from the recent harvest. In one corner was a little bamboo platform on which the parents and three small children slept. But the children were wide awake as we entered, staring at their mother who half-lay, half-sat against the wall, her tongue hanging from her mouth. She was evidently very sick.

"What's the matter with her?" I asked as I jumped up on the platform by her side.

"The evil spirits have possessed her," her husband answered in a low voice filled with horror.

The flickering light from two candles cast shadows over the rice. As I looked around the room, I saw that it resembled a stable full of hay more than a home. I reached over and touched the woman's forehead. She felt hot.

"When did she last eat?" I asked her husband.

He told me that they had eaten rice for breakfast the day before. But last night, they had been too tired from laboring in the hot sun all day to beat the husks off the newly harvested rice in order to cook it. They had not stopped for lunch, either, because they were trying to save the rice before it rained again.

His wife had been carrying her year-old baby on her back while she worked in the field. At the end of the day, they just fell asleep, planning to beat the husk off the rice at daybreak to have some food for breakfast. But now she seemed to be in a semi-coma.

I had no idea what to do, so while Ken prayed with them, I rushed home, pulled my cooking stones together, started a fire and boiled some water to cook some thin oatmeal. Returning to the neighbor's hut, I had to force the oatmeal into the young woman's mouth. After swallowing some, her stiff body relaxed and she leaned over in my arms. "They have gone," she murmured, hardly above a whisper.

"Who has gone?" I asked her.

"All those women who were trying to carry me off."

After finishing the dish of oatmeal, she fell asleep. We stayed with the father a while longer until he, too, was calmer and the children were sleeping. I don't know what kind of an attack the woman had that night, but I was thankful that she did not die.

Marta, after she was well again, weaving a blanket out of thread spun from her cotton tree.

Later, as Ken and I walked home under the stars, I realized again that we had indeed come to a land of opportunity, but also a land of ignorance and disease, of suffering and death, a land of people with big hearts, willing to share with others their blessings as well as their sorrows.

(opposite page)
Installing the drain in one of the fish ponds
Ken, in front; Sato, next in line behind him; Fermin, beside pipe

Chapter Seven

The Fish Project

"We have here only five loaves of bread and two fish....Bring them here to me," Jesus said. And he directed the people to sit down on the grass. Taking the five loaves and the two fish and looking up to heaven, he gave thanks and broke the loaves.... They all ate and were satisfied.

—Matthew 14:17-20

What is protein?" asked one of the *hermanos* at a town meeting in February. This question followed a discussion of why so many of the children were sickly and often died.

"Protein is found in meat, fish, milk and eggs. When beans are mixed with rice, they have protein too. We must have protein for our bodies to grow and stay healthy," Ken replied. "Without protein, we will get sick and eventually die."

The men were disturbed. "But you know we don't have much milk or meat. There are only three cows in all of the area...and the vampire bats suck the blood from our hens while they sleep and keep them too anemic to lay many eggs."

There used to be fish in our little creek, too, but the bigger ones had "gotten away"— exterminated by the early settlers who had used dynamite to catch them.

The Alto Beni was the first place in Latin America we had lived where the people did not have beans to eat with their rice. Their diet was greatly deficient in protein, but many had not even realized what protein was or that they needed it. Now they were worried. "What can we do?" they asked Ken.

As facilitators for community development in areas like the Alto Beni, we had learned not to answer questions the people did not ask; rather, to live with them in such a way that they would ask the questions that could help them develop. Once they asked, we knew they would be interested enough to consider our answer, and we would not be simply imposing our suggestions on their circumstances.

Ken had studied fish culture and had longed to start a fish project in Sapecho, but he waited until asked for his advice. "Fish ponds take a long time to dig, but once you have a pond, fish are easier to raise than cows or pigs."

There was a buzz as the *hermanos* discussed this concept among themselves. Then one of them asked Ken, "If we make a project to raise fish, would you help us with it?"

Ken picked up on the key word *we*. The *hermano* had said, "If *we* make a fish project...." This was the opening Ken had been waiting for. A project that was their idea from the beginning would have a much better chance of succeeding.

He, of course, agreed and the vote was unanimous. To accomplish this ambitious project, the people would tax themselves twenty days of labor per family. The town of Sapecho donated eight urban lots to the church to be used for a nursery to grow the baby fish to be distributed to families who would dig their own ponds.

Ken told them about the DNOCS program in Forteleza, Brazil, a program carried out jointly by the Brazilian government, USAid and Auburn University Fisheries, where we might get the breeding stock for tilapia. They asked Ken to put Sapecho on the waiting list for the beginning stock.

While some fish require high-protein food, tilapia are omnivorous and can survive on algae created from manure or rotten fruit in a pond. They also propagate so rapidly that a small pond is soon so full of fish, none of them can grow to be large. But since these people were accustomed to eating small fish, even minnows, the homesteaders would keep netting the smaller fish out and eat them in their soup, allowing the others to grow larger.

With a waiting list for the fingerlings, which are distributed to many tropical countries, Ken was surprised when the village of Sapecho was given an early date of May 17 to receive our first fish. The entire community was excited about the project, and I overheard one small child telling another, "Fish has protein in it, and we're going to get some!"

After months of planning, obtaining the

necessary permissions from various government offices, and digging, it appeared that the project would become a reality by the end of April. We felt that if individual fish ponds became widespread in this area, it would mean a big difference in the diet of the people. Children who were suffering and dying from malnutrition would have a better chance to live. We hoped to follow in the footsteps of Jesus, who multiplied two small fish and fed a multitude.

Miracle of Miracles

For us, the entire project was one miracle after another. The first was the fact that Ken was given permission to bring the fish into the country after the Peace Corps had been denied six years earlier.

It was another miracle that we were able to obtain a bulldozer to dig the original four breeding ponds, for few bulldozers are available in Bolivia. After spending several days going from one government office to another, Ken found one man who would listen—the director of all roads in the region. This man had a small bulldozer going in to build a country road near us and was willing to lend it to us for two weeks, free of charge!

After the bulldozer left, there remained days

and days of work to finish drains and lay topsoil over the floor of the ponds. Everyone realized it would take the whole community working together to get the ponds finished by the time the fish were scheduled to arrive. During this time, our family had been beset by serious illnesses. Part of the time, Ken was out working with pick and shovel when he should have been in bed.

Perhaps the greatest miracle was that all the homesteaders in the village—its population composed of Spanish, mestizos, and four different indigenous tribes, with their differing customs and languages—came together to work in harmony for the good of all.

One day in early May before sunrise, Ken and I walked over to the ponds, hardly daring to believe what we saw in the early morning light. "We only lack the finishing touches," I said, my voice trembling with excitement.

Ken's eyes were misty. "This is not our doing," he said. "This whole project has been a miracle from God."

Fish Project in Peril

To our dismay, only a week later, we

discovered that the project was far from completion. To complete the project as recommended by the experts in Brazil, we needed four fish ponds.

When we started to pump the water from the nearby stream to fill the ponds, however, we discovered a leak in the drain about six feet below the surface of the ground in one of the ponds. Ken and the village men would have to re-dig this deep ditch, fix the leak and re-pack the clay on top of it. It was a big setback, especially since we were working against a deadline. Ken had to leave at the end of the week to go to Brazil to get the fingerlings, and he didn't want to leave until the ponds were finished.

The cry for "all hands on deck" rang out. Neighbors, *hermanos,* even the women and children came out to dig. All of us worked at breakneck speed, trying to overcome one setback after another. Every night we re-calculated: Five more days to work…four more…three. Could we possibly get the ponds finished and filled with water in time?

By Wednesday we knew that it would be impossible to complete the job during the daylight hours, so we kept working after dark with the aid of torches and candlelight. We hauled rocks from the creek and then mixed and poured the cement around the drain of one pond, finishing late into the night.

"Now if all goes well from here on," Ken began, as we wearily sat down late that night to eat the supper Kathy had prepared for us, "we have a chance to make it."

But he had not counted on the terrible rainstorm that came the following night.

This is what happened the night of the flood, as told in Ken's words:

Soon after midnight on the one-hundredth day of our stay in Sapecho, the sky opened up with a tropical downpour of ferocious intensity. About 3:30 A.M., Sato, our twenty-two-year-old, next-door neighbor, who had worked with us constantly in this project, woke us up to warn us that the water pump was in danger of being carried away by the swollen stream or buried by the dam, which was a mountain of fresh-piled dirt looming above it—now a dangerous mass of saturated clay.

That pump was our prized possession. Without it, there was no hope of filling the ponds, for the stream was some twenty-five feet below the top of the dam. Chris had made a special trip all the way to La Paz to purchase it when friends in the States had made funds available. We could not lose the pump!

Lightning was flashing, lighting up the jungle at the edge of the fish ponds, and the thunder was deafening. But Chris pulled on his clothes, grabbed a flashlight, and plunged out into the storm.

"'I'll get it!' he called back, but Sato was right behind him. 'You can't do it alone! I've tried already, but between us, I think we can!'

Barely able to walk in the slippery clay and scarcely able to see by flashlight through the heavy rain, the boys began the descent of the dangerous mountain of mud, aware that at any minute they could be buried alive. They also realized the danger of the flash-flood waters, ripping down the narrow canyon that contains the little stream. They could literally be drowned as they bogged down in the quagmire or be carried downstream to the now raging Beni River, a short mile below. Though the very real danger was in the back of their minds, both Chris and Sato were determined to save the new pump.

When they reached the swollen stream, they realized that the thirty meters of two-inch PVC pipe that stretched up over the high dam above the pump was immovable, and they had no tools to work with. Now Chris must again ascend the treacherous mass of mud to get a hacksaw to cut off the pipe and free it from the pump.

As he started back down with the saw, he took only one step before miring up to his hip in mud. He fell flat on his back, and in struggling to regain a standing position, began to slide. He slid all the way down the mud bank on his back, stopping at the edge of the stream near the pump where Sato waited. It didn't take long to cut the pipe off, and together they struggled back up the bank with the pump.

The next day, work at the pump site was impossible. When I would start to lift a foot to take a step, my boot would stick in the mud, and I would almost fall. Our chickens could barely navigate with the weight of mud on their feet and had to flap their wings to walk.

But the countdown didn't stop because of the mud. Two more days to go. Could we possibly get the ponds finished and filled in time? At the pace we had been working, it took more than a day and night to fill each pond after it was repaired. We felt that the lives of many children, now and in the future, might depend on our meeting this deadline to bring more protein to the Alto Beni.

The Struggle Continues

The four ponds were ready the very day that Ken was scheduled to leave for Brazil. This trip was necessary since the Center in Brazil had required two people from the village to take a two-week course in raising tilapia before giving them the fingerlings. The course was given in Portuguese or in English. None of the *hermanos* knew either language, so they elected Chris to go with Ken. Ken was disturbed, however, that two of the ponds had developed a minor leak, but the brothers of the church assured him they could fix the leaks in his absence. No worries.

When Ken and Chris left, the rest of our family also left Sapecho for various scheduled church retreats. Sato had worked with the fish project from the beginning and would take care of the ponds while we were gone.

All was well…or so we thought.

Late Friday evening, six days later, Karen and I returned to Sapecho to be greeted with more bad news. "Water is still escaping from two of the four ponds," Sato explained. "We have tried everything we know, but the water pours out as fast as we can pump it in."

Sato showed me the problem ponds and I realized that the *hermanos* had done everything humanly possible. "There's only one person on this side of the big river who can help us," I told Sato. "The district road engineer who loaned us the bulldozer for the ponds could tell us what to do."

"But there is no *mobilidad*, no transportation to get to him," Sato objected. He was right. No one in our whole town owned a vehicle and the engineer was in Palos Blancos, ten kilometers away.

When we needed to get from one place to another, we had always hitched rides on the supply trucks, but they rarely traveled at night.

"How can we get to the engineer in time?" Sato continued. "He will leave for work early in the morning. It would be late tomorrow night before you could contact him."

"But if we could reach him tonight...?"

"Hermana," Sato interrupted me, "I have to keep the pump filled with gasoline to pump the water in...I cannot leave it. We are running out of time to get these two ponds filled. It's almost dark now...how could you travel ten kilometers through the jungle on foot?"

I had walked the jungle roads at night before. It was not dangerous, but it was scary, especially wading the creeks. Yet that was the only way to save the ponds. Any of the *hermanos* would have been willing to go, but I knew that the elite Spanish engineer was prejudiced against the indigenous people and would not take kindly to one of them disturbing his rest. I also knew he respected Americans—my husband in particular—so I was the logical one to make the trek.

Karen insisted on going with me, so we set out walking, jogging, running, trying to reach the next village some ten kilometers (six miles) distant before the engineer went to bed. I was very proud of our ten-year-old Karen. She assumed a calm neither she nor I felt. We both were tired from our long trip home from La Paz before we started our journey, but we scarcely noticed. All we heard and felt were the calls of the wild animals and the birds screeching in the woods around us. The jungle comes alive at night! Our flashlight began to grow dim and we faced the possibility that we'd be finishing our trip in darkness.

We had walked almost two hours when we heard the *mobilidad.* A truck was coming! What a miracle! Sure enough it stopped for us, and we climbed on back, too thankful for words. The driver took us within a few yards of the engineer's home.

Although the engineer was a busy man, he agreed to help. Right away, he brought us home in his truck and examined the ponds by flashlight. "We can remedy this," he said. "If you can have four men here early in the morning, I will explain to them what to do before I go to work."

Sato and I spoke in unison. "The men will be here!"

Willing Workers

During the rice harvest, every available hand is busy trying to save the rice—the staple crop for the Alto Beni. The homesteaders had thought they had finished the fish ponds and now they were working hard to save their rice before the next rains. It was almost midnight. How could we find four men ready to donate a day's work by early morning?

Leaving Karen at home to sleep, Sato refilled the pump with gasoline, and we started out on our search. We walked two kilometers down the road to the home of Abdon Paredes, the lay leader of the church.

"Hermano!" we called until he awoke and sleepily came to the door with a candle in his hand. We explained our predicament around the table in his little thatched-roof house. The candle flickered, but even in the dim light, we could see the determination in his eyes.

"My rice can wait, even if I lose it," he declared. "I will be there in the morning with three others. If four men is all you need, go home and get some sleep, *Hermanos.* I can find them for you."

It seemed we had scarcely laid our heads

down before it was time to be up again. Before daylight, Sato was pumping water—out of the pond this time—making preparations for the engineer to show them how to repair it. Soon Abdon came and, with him, not four but nine more men.

The engineer was impressed. "If these people want to work, I will help them," he said. He showed them what to do before leaving for his own job.

All day they worked hard, excavating the two-meter-deep drainage ditch. The engineer returned in the late afternoon, bringing his compacting machine to pack it well. He also brought tar, and just as it was getting dark, melted the tar and sealed the stopper on the drainage tube—and the third pond was ready for water. Only one more pond to go...and we had another whole week to fix the last one before the fish arrived!

◊

The next day, Sunday, brought another terrible rainstorm. The engineer came by in the rain just before our church service started, and looked at the ponds. "I am sorry to have to tell you," he said, "but the soil around this last pond is so wet, it cannot be worked until at least the last of the week. There is no way this soil can dry in time to have the pond ready for the fish Saturday. We have all tried, but we are going to have to give up now. Wet soil cannot be compacted. It is impossible. And, look, the rain keeps coming down. Who knows when this storm will pass?"

Abdon thanked the engineer for his help, then added, "But, sir, we can't give up. We have worked four months on this fish project. We will just leave it in God's hands, and whatever He does will be all right."

That Sunday, our church service was mainly a prayer meeting. The people poured out their hearts to God about the fish project. These long-suffering people knew what it was to work hard and then see everything washed away. They told God that if they lost the fish project, they would not complain, but they hoped He would save it for them.

By the time the service was over, the storm had passed. The sun came out, hotter than ever, and shone down on us all day. On Monday, the sun continued to shine.

On Tuesday, the engineer came back and

squeezed some soil into a ball in his hand. "This is amazing!" he exclaimed. "I have never known soil to dry so fast. I believe this soil can be worked. We just might make it by Saturday, after all."

With praise in their hearts and half the town of Sapecho by his side, the people went to work on the last pond. They worked frantically, even digging out the mud with their bare hands when there were not enough shovels. At midnight on Tuesday, the engineer declared that the fourth pond was ready for water.

It was a happy moment when we gathered in my kitchen for a hot drink of the strong, locally grown chocolate, all of us covered in mud, before returning to our various homes. Now maybe we could breathe a deep sigh of relief....

"Don't Be Dismayed"

Wednesday was late to send a radiogram to Ken, but with luck he would get it. So Karen and I started out once again, this time to the home of the Caufields, the missionaries across the river, to radio a message to him. "I can say 'Four ponds ready'," I happily told Sato as we were leaving.

But Sato looked troubled. "If we had

another hose so that we could use this other borrowed pump, we could say that. But there's no way our one pump can finish filling these four ponds by Saturday."

I had been so concerned with repairing the ponds that I had forgotten how long it took to pump the water. Now I was numb with exhaustion. "We've done all we can do," I replied with resignation. "There's not another two-inch PVC pipe in the whole Alto Beni, especially not one that is thirty meters long. We can't use the borrowed pump without a hose. Now we've reached the last obstacle, and there's no way we can overcome it."

But *Hermano* Abdon's words from Sunday kept coming to my mind. "We can pray!" I was convinced that prayer had brought the engineer and the neighbors and had enabled us to fix the ponds. But what good were empty ponds when the fish would be here soon? How could God suddenly provide us with a two-inch-wide hose thirty meters long out in the middle of the jungle?

"Go on across the river," Sato counseled. "Pastor Ken is waiting for the radiogram today to know how things are here. If you don't send it, he will be worried. And there's nothing else you can do here. I'll keep our little pump going."

Karen and I set out for the Caufields's, ten miles away. We caught a big truck part of the way, but it was so old, the driver barely crept along. At every bump in the road, the ancient vehicle shook and rattled and banged us against the sides. Then it would stop. It took us two hours to travel the ten miles. All the way, as I held onto the side of the truck, the words of the song the Aymarans sang at church kept going through my head:

Dear Brother, don't be dismayed.
Jesus Christ is at your side.
I'll follow Him. You follow Him.
Let's all follow Jesus, our Savior.

Yes, Lord, I prayed silently, *I will follow You! But I give up on saving the fish ponds. I can't even ask You for a thirty-meter-long PVC pipe here in the jungle. I guess I don't believe that You just hand things like that down from the sky. We wanted to help these wonderful, hard-working homesteaders provide food for their children. But we are about to fail. Three ponds are not enough, Lord. But You love these dear people. Help them, Lord. If it's done, You will have to do it!*

The words of the song continued to play through my mind as I held on, so tired I would doze off until the next bump woke me with a start.

It was late afternoon when we arrived at the Caufields's house. There we found Tommy and Kathy, who had hitchhiked back from the capital after a retreat in the church there. They had many things to tell us.

"But, first, how are the ponds?" everyone asked.

I shook my head sadly. "The ponds are all repaired, but there's no way we can get them filled in time for the fish unless we find a two-inch-wide PVC hose—and soon."

"What a shame," Rosa Caufield sympathized. "If only we had one to lend you, but there is no hose that size this side of La Paz."

"I'm too tired to feel our failure," I groaned. "I just want to sit here and not move for hours."

At that moment, from where Rosa and I were sitting—looking into their bedroom door and through the bedroom window—she caught sight of something and gasped. "What is that sticking up at the bottom of the window? Isn't it a two-inch hose of some kind?"

We rushed outside and, sure enough, a thick roll of PVC hose was leaning against the Caufields's house. "The people who finished the water project here in Kilometer 73 must have left it! They came back looking for it and couldn't find it. They thought it had been stolen and gave it up for lost, but some worker had just put it here out of the way. I can't tell you how many times I've passed this window since they were here," she said, her eyes wide, "and I never noticed it before."

What miracle would God work next?! I didn't measure the big roll of pipe leaning against their house, but I knew without a doubt it would be at least thirty meters long. Rosa's husband, Bob, was away in their jeep and there was no *mobilidad* to carry the hose and me the two kilometers to Puerto Linares, where the trucks crossed the ferry. Would there be a truck there I could rent?

Every minute counted. Even if we had the hose in place at that very moment, already there was not enough time left to fill the pond as full as it needed to be before Ken and Chris arrived with the fish. But maybe it would be enough to keep them alive…if we hurried. I began to run toward Puerto Linares. I forgot I was tired. I ran faster than I knew I could. God had given us the hose, right there in the middle of the jungle. Now it was my job to move it the ten miles to Sapecho. *Please, dear God! Let there be a truck!*

Darkness was descending as I ran into the little settlement at the river's edge. There was not a single vehicle in town. *No mobilidad!* I slumped down on a log by the river to catch my breath, very close to tears. So near and yet so far.

When I peered across the river in the semi-darkness, there was the most beautiful sight I could imagine! Parked in the middle of the road was the dilapidated old pick-up used to transport people back and forth from the river inland several times a week, much like a bus service. Even though the owner called it the *Servicio Rápido,* it was slow and barely held together, but tonight it looked like a chariot fit for a king!

Jumping up, I pulled out a coin and ran to the nearest canoe taxi. "The other side!" I yelled. "Quick!" The canoe leaped into the river as the owner tried to please. Barely thanking him after reaching the other side, I jumped out and ran to the old truck.

"Hermano," I pleaded, "please turn your truck around and come with me back across the river to Kilometer 73!"

"But, Sister, it's getting dark," the owner objected. "You know it's against the law for the ferry to cross at night. They won't take me."

"Will you go if the Captain of the Navy gives permission?"

He agreed, so I jumped into another canoe taxi and dashed back across the river to Puerto Linares to the small bamboo hut, which served as the Naval headquarters for the area. Rushing in, I asked the soldiers for the captain.

"He's in the bar, back on the other side of the river," they told me.

With the help of another canoe taxi, I crossed the big river again and ran into the bamboo bar perched on stilts beside the water. "I need the Captain of the Navy! It's urgent!" I called out to all the men in the bar.

"He just left," came the unwelcome reply. "He just went back to the Naval office. You must have crossed each other on the river in the dark."

Wasting no time, I was soon crossing again, and this time ran breathlessly into the Naval Center. There he was, the aloof Spanish officer who controlled all the rivers—and the people of this region.

"Captain, Captain!" I gasped. Having found him at last, suddenly I couldn't talk, I couldn't breathe, I simply burst into tears. I was furious with myself that all the weight of the last days and the lack of sleep had left me unable to say a word when I most needed my communication skills. I just sobbed. *Now he will never help me*, I thought.

But he quickly pulled out a chair and graciously offered it to me. "Here, Señora, rest and catch your breath. Nothing can be that bad. When you are calm, I will hear your problem. Whatever it is, I will help you. Anything you need."

Suddenly my tears dried up, and I blurted out, "Give permission for the ferry to cross the river."

"Oh, that is the one thing I *cannot* do," he replied. "It is against the law to take a vehicle across the river at night." It was common knowledge that the dictator of the country was determined to keep track of the people's movements in order to repress any potential uprising. "I could never let a vehicle cross the river after dark." The captain's tone was firm, authoritative...and final.

I explained to him our great need and added, "Now after four months of struggle, we will lose the fish project if you don't give permission to cross tonight. Sir, you said you would do anything to help me."

"That's right, Captain," a marine spoke up. "You told the lady you would do anything to help her." The other sailors nodded.

He hesitated, then reluctantly agreed. "All right, I will give you fifteen minutes to get that truck over here, load the hose, and get back over on the other side again. Only fifteen minutes!"

"Thank you! Thank you!" I yelled over my shoulder as I ran toward another canoe taxi. Approaching the other side, I called out to the owner of the Servicio Rápido, "Come on, *Hermano!* The Captain said *yes!*"

"But, Sister, I don't have any lights, and it's dark," he argued. "I only said I would go because I knew the Captain wouldn't permit it."

"Please, Brother, we can go by flashlight tonight!" As the ferry pulled into place to receive the old truck, the driver hesitantly started the engine, and I made my sixth crossing that evening—but this time with a *mobilidad.*

At the Caufields's house, we grabbed the hose, and, leaving Kathy, Tommy and Karen to visit with Steve and Jennine Caufield, set off in great haste for the ferry two miles away. I held my flashlight out the window, but it didn't have much effect in the deep darkness. There was no moon, yet that old truck must have had a short in the electrical system, because when we hit a big bump, the lights would flash on for a few seconds…on and off…again and again. Each time we were near a dangerous drop-off or a big curve, they popped on, and we were able to make it all the way to Sapecho without incident.

As we pulled up alongside the fish ponds, suddenly the truck's headlights came on again. For a moment we could see all the neighbors praying around the empty fish pond. It was a sight I will never forget.

Sato and other neighbors came running and, without a word, rushed to hook up the other pump. We would run both pumps all night and up until the time Ken and Chris arrived tomorrow. That should be enough water to save the fish. The hose we had found at the Caufields's place was just long enough to reach the pond from the pump.

"Incredible!" Sato said in a voice that was barely audible. There were tears in our eyes as we watched the water pour into both ponds at the same time. I had to strain to hear his words, as he spoke again. "The hose is exactly to the inch what we needed to finish this project, and God prepared it for us when the workers in Kilometer 73 left it five months ago!"

Zero Hour

I wish I did not have to reveal the next incident in this long saga, because I feel so badly about what we did. But to be truthful, I must.

That night Sato was almost asleep on his feet. Neither of us had slept more than two hours a night all week, but he had rested less than I. "Tonight is my turn to keep the pumps going," I insisted.

Since my children were still at the Caufields's place and not there to help me, Sato's twelve-year-old nephew, Luis, came to stay with me as we waited the night out on the edge of the ponds. Luis and I talked and walked around to keep ourselves awake. Since we had not stopped for supper earlier, we built a fire and I cooked some eggs.

At 1:30 A.M., we had to re-fill the pumps with gas. Almost asleep, Luis and I stumbled down the steep bank to the creek, carrying the gas in a plastic jug. Luis checked the oil, then picked up a plastic jug and filled both the pumps while I watched. But afterward, neither pump would start.

"Maybe I filled them too full and flooded them," Luis suggested. "I'll siphon some out."

But when he tasted the liquid, the look on his face was unforgettable. *"Hermana!"* he exclaimed. "This is not gasoline…it's water! I've filled the tanks with *water!*"

For the first time, I noticed some water jugs near the pumps, the same kind of jugs that held our gasoline. He had picked up the wrong jug, and I had stood there and watched him do it!

Luis and I worked fast. We cleaned the tanks and took apart every moveable part, trying to get all the water out. I knew so little about motors, I felt ridiculous trying to fix the pumps. Here God had provided us with the hose to fill the ponds, and Luis and I had messed the whole thing up.

At 4:30 A.M., we gave up and I slept for about an hour. Then I was up again, ready to catch any truck that came out early, going back to Puerto Linares. I just wanted to get my children, come home, and forget I had ever heard of fish!

But God was in my path again. As I walked into Puerto Linares at 8 A.M., there was the Peace Corps worker from Holland in her jeep. "How are the ponds?" she asked. Quite ashamed, I told her what had happened.

"My friend here is a mechanic. We'll go help you," she offered.

I could hardly believe there was hope again. Mechanics are hard to find in an area like the Alto

Beni. I jumped in her jeep and we were on our way back to Sapecho. He was able to repair only one of the pumps. But he told me of a mechanic in Palos Blancos, the next town farther inland, who could probably fix the other one.

By 11 A.M., pump in hand, Luis and I hitched a ride on a truck. It took that mechanic till dark to get the pump started. We were fortunate to hitch a ride home that night since there were so few vehicles on the road.

But when we got home with the pump, it wouldn't start again. Sato and I worked on that pump until 2 A.M., when I gave up again and went to bed. I thought he was going to bed too.

At 5 A.M., while it was still dark, I awoke and glanced toward the ponds. I was shocked into action. There was a fire below the dam, down near the pumps. *Now the one good pump has caught on fire while we slept!* I thought as I raced toward it.

But when I reached the dam, there sat Sato, hunched over a fire he had built to keep warm in the night. Both pumps were working just fine.

I slid down the bank. "Sato! I thought you were going to bed!"

He grinned shyly. "Look," he said. "God

helped me fix the pump." The automatic valve wasn't working right. He had propped a screwdriver on it and weighed it down with a file. If he had used pliers or any other tool, it wouldn't have worked. But the file was just the right weight. We both wept then, maybe with joy, maybe from nervous exhaustion.

I returned and grated some of the local chocolate, mixed it with water and sugar, and took it down to Sato's fire to heat for our breakfast. We knew for sure that the ponds would be ready. Our only concern now was that the fish would survive the long trip across the continent.

The ponds are finally ready for the fingerlings.

The Fish Arrive

While we were struggling nearly twenty-two hours a day to repair the damaged ponds and fill them with water, Ken and Chris, in Brazil and unaware of our problems, were taking a two-week course on fish culture.

The DNOCS Fisheries in Forteleza, where they studied, was one of the largest tropical food fish research stations in the world. The many acres of fish ponds of all sizes were maintained by the Brazilian government, with aid from the United States government and with the technical and research personnel provided by Auburn University. Ken felt proud to be from Alabama when he saw what Auburn was doing with tropical fish there. Dr. Leonard Lovshin directed their course. Not only did Ken and Chris study theory, but they also worked in the fisheries, learning the process from start to finish.

DNOCS Fisheries is on the opposite side of Brazil from Bolivia, and Brazil is a huge country. It would take ten hours flying time to return to La Paz, in addition to a four-hour layover in Rio de Janeiro.

When they were leaving, one of the leaders

of the fisheries took them to the airport. In parting, Ken commented, "You have a marvelous facility here. What great opportunities you have to make tremendous strides in protein production, with the Brazilian government, the United States government and Auburn University behind you."

The scientist encouraged Ken with his response. "Yes, we have many resources. And you do too. You have God!"

Chris, in Brazil, studying how to raise fish
before bringing fingerlings back to Sapecho

The major concern on the return flight was the welfare of the fish that had been placed in plastic bags with only a little water and some oxygen that had been pumped into the bags before departure. But it was a risky transfer.

At the airport in La Paz, the Bolivian Air Force was waiting to fly Ken and Chris and their precious cargo down the Andes to the Alto Beni in a four-seater Cessna. The twelve-hour bus ride, with all those twists and turns, would have been pushing the fish too far. Not only that, but the lives of the little fish were in danger from the high altitude and cold in La Paz.

"I'll fly as low as I have ever flown," the pilot offered. "It will be better for the fish."

Ken assured me that the pilot did exactly that—flew as low as anyone could ever fly down the deep ravines and precipices of the snow-covered Andes. In one place, they had to fly through a narrow pass because the peaks on either side were too high to risk flying over. Ken and Chris declared that if they had stuck their hand out the window, they could have scooped up snow.

Meanwhile back at the fish ponds, all four of them were finally ready to receive the fish. Kathy, Tommy, Karen and I hitchhiked the ten kilometers to the pasture that runs along the side of the Beni River. The pilot would use this for the landing strip. At 4:30 we heard the little plane and saw it line up for a landing.

Two passing mules chose that moment to break away from their owner and run toward the airstrip. We prayed as we watched in horror. The mules raced down the runway, dragging a log behind them, right in the path of the descending plane. Just as the plane touched down, they jumped to one side and ran out of the way, with only seconds to spare!

Ken and Chris arrive by plane with the fingerlings...just in time!

Chris, then Ken, climbed out, carefully holding the Styrofoam boxes containing the plastic bags with the little fish inside. Bob Caufield was there in his jeep to rush us to Sapecho, for each minute in the plastic bags was stressing the fingerlings more. Dr. Lovshin had said there would be enough oxygen for the fish to be safe until 3:30 that day. But it was now 5:30 when we drove into Sapecho in a cloud of dust.

Seeing the jeep approach, the townspeople ran behind us. The crowd of eager spectators watched as Ken opened the Styrofoam boxes and took out the plastic bags inside. We all stood by as Ken held the bags in the pond until the water temperature gradually equalized. Then one by one, he took out each small fish, examined it, then turned it loose in the pond water. All fifty-six fish were alive! Four were missing a piece of their tails, but otherwise appeared healthy.

We had faced unbelievable obstacles in turning a jungle into a fish farm. Time after time, when we had reached our limit, God moved beyond our expectations. Many people had worked together to help. On two different occasions, when men were not on speaking terms with each other, they were reconciled in the process of working closely together day after day.

After the last fish swam out of Ken's hand, he stood to thank the people who had given so much of their time at great sacrifice. There were tears in many eyes as we saw the dream beginning to become a reality. As twilight settled over the Alto Beni, we bowed our heads in a community prayer with our neighbors around the fish ponds and thanked God for His great provision. And now, like Jesus with the loaves and fishes, we prayed that He would once again multiply the fish to feed all the hungry families in the Alto Beni.

Ken, examining each fingerling
before releasing the fish into the ponds

(opposite page)

The people of the Alto Beni sacrificed their time
to help build our home, their church and their community.

Chapter Eight

Others Join the Work

Whatever you do, work at it with all your heart....
It is the Lord Christ you are serving.
—Colossians 3:23, 24

The fish were safe in their ponds. The rice was harvested. Winter was beginning, which meant pleasant, spring-like weather in the Alto Beni. The stress of the last few months was behind us, and the people were ready to celebrate with a week of special services in the church.

From all over the Alto Beni, the people gathered at our little church in Sapecho, walking or hitching rides on supply trucks. The first to arrive was a man who had walked two days in the rain and mud. Everyone brought a blanket, which also served as their "bed," and at night the schoolhouse and the church were turned into dormitories. In a corner of the church yard, big stones were set up to hold pots for cooking.

All the *hermanos* in Sapecho brought donations of their farm products to be used in feeding the visitors who came from afar. One corner of our back porch was piled high with green bananas covered with leaves so that they would ripen in time. Our little house was filled with bags of rice, potatoes, yuca and another grain called quinoa, which someone had brought down from the Altiplano.

One of the *hermanos* had made a drink called *chicha* from boiled, ground fresh corn, which was strained and then sweetened. It is customary to let this drink ferment to make a kind of home brew, but the Bolivian Methodists did not drink alcohol, so this *chicha* was fresh. Since containers were always scarce, my new plastic garbage cans, which had not yet been used, held the *chicha*.

One man brought chocolate, which he had grown and processed himself. And the only nearby homesteader who owned a cow donated all the milk his cow gave during the revival. To stretch it so that there would be enough to go around, the cook mixed water with the milk so we even had hot chocolate for breakfast—a rare treat.

After breakfast, Bible studies and spontaneous praise services began and lasted till noon. It was no trouble to get the dishes washed, for each person washed his own bowl, spoon and cup. At noon, we ate and talked for two hours, after which the Bible classes started again and finished around 5 P.M.

Following supper, we had another service. The people could not get enough Bible teaching and worship. Many of them came from villages where there were no churches or pastors, with few opportunities to hear a sermon. And since so many could not read, they were dependent upon someone else telling them what the Bible says. They would even gather informally at rest periods to continue the hymn-singing. During the revival, seventeen adults made decisions to become Christians.

Since Sunday morning was the final service

of the week, we circled the fish ponds to dedicate them to the glory of God. Ken preached, after many of the *hermanos* made speeches of gratitude to God for the safe arrival of the fish and for the spirit of unity shown by the entire community, as they worked tirelessly to build the ponds.

And then the last two *hermanos* in the village who were not on speaking terms, came forward at the last service and publicly asked each other's forgiveness. As they wept and embraced, their wives also came forward to forgive each other for past hurts. It was a beautiful climax to the fish project and to the revival.

Little did we know at that moment how important these two men—Abdon and Benjo (pronounced Ben-Ho) Paredes—would become to the development of the kingdom of God in the Alto Beni.

Benjamin "Benjo" Paredes

I'll never forget the first time we met Benjo Paredes. That is, the first time *Ken* met Benjo...less than a week after we moved to the Alto Beni.

The scorching sun was beating down with fierce intensity as Ken drove a jeep, borrowed from the church, down the little dirt road leading from the river to Sapecho. When he noticed an indigenous man walking on the side of the road, carrying a heavy load on his back, Ken stopped to ask if he wanted a ride. It was years later, when I was translating for Benjo during a visit to the U.S., before we knew what he had been feeling that day.

After planting many types of beans, Benjo prepares them for market.

He looked up into Ken's face and saw everything he hated—a white man, American, powerful, surely the oppressor. Benjo wanted to spit in that face, but the sun was relentless and he had almost ten miles to go…so he accepted the ride. Ken explained that he was the new pastor, although Benjo had surmised as much. Expecting Ken to "hit him over the head with the Bible," so to speak, Benjo was surprised when Ken merely asked, "What can I do to help in Sapecho?"

Because the people who had called themselves "Christians" where Benjo had grown up did not want street children in their churches, he was surprised by this Christian's offer. During their ten-mile ride, the two men discussed the needs of Sapecho and what could be done to help the homesteaders lift themselves out of poverty. Benjo realized that he had found a friend who truly cared about the poor.

On the other hand, Ken learned that Benjamin Paredes served as one of the main leaders in the Alto Beni, holding such volunteer positions as mayor of Sapecho and district president of the Parent/Teacher Association. He had already led the homesteaders in founding Ceibo, a cacao cooperative so that they could cut out the middle man and market their own chocolate products. Today, some thirty-five years later, this cooperative is stronger than ever and helps the cacao farmers receive a just wage for their labor.

Benjo's insight and leadership gave hope to the illiterate and semi-literate homesteaders that someday their hard work would pay off. Even though he himself had very little formal education, Benjo understood life issues, such as root causes of some of their problems, creative ways of eliminating them, and what they could produce that would bring the largest return.

He began to visit Ken every evening after work, and often stayed late at night as they brainstormed ideas as to how to alleviate some of the suffering in their village. Later, when the community asked Ken to help them with the fish project, Benjo was involved from the beginning.

"Stars Above Me"

After that project, Benjo stayed at our home even later in the evenings, asking more questions, which meant I couldn't go to bed until he left, since our living room and bedroom were the same. So I sat quietly in one corner, praying as the men talked.

One night Benjo asked Ken, "Why do you care about the poor?"

Ken and I had learned not to answer a question people did not ask, but to live in such a way that they would want to know what we had to share. Like the fish project, this was another of those teachable moments. Ken opened the Bible to Matthew 25 and read the story Jesus told about the last judgment. Those who feed the hungry are feeding Him; those who give water to the thirsty or care for the sick and imprisoned are doing it for Him. And those who do not do these good deeds are withholding them from Him. Those words are just as true today as when Jesus first spoke them to His disciples, and they were true for Benjo that day in Bolivia....

Benjo was amazed. From his childhood experiences, he had decided that if there were a God, He was the god of the rich. What Ken was saying was the very opposite of all Benjo believed. Ken further told him that God loves everyone and has commanded us to love even our enemies and those who mistreat us. To Benjo, that was a revelation, the absolute antithesis of his worldview.

The following evening sessions were filled with Benjo's questions about the Bible and what it meant to follow Jesus. One night after midnight, he left our house and walked out into the darkness to the middle of the four fish ponds. He stood there, gazing up at the stars reflected in the ponds. "Stars above me, stars below me," he later told us in describing that time.

"Suddenly I knew that I wanted Jesus more than anything else in the world," he said. "I realized that all my resentment and hatred for those who had abused me as a child were wrong. I fell on my knees and poured out my heart to God, begging His forgiveness, asking Him to make me clean, to help me to love like that so I could really help my people."

In the stillness of that dark, star-spangled night, Benjo felt the presence of Jesus and knew he would never be the same. The next evening he came back and told Ken, "I am really ready to work with you now, Pastor. I have become a Christian!"

God of the Rich?

True to his word, Benjo continued to volunteer as much time as he could manage and still keep his farm going. As he worked side by side with us in community projects, from time to time he would share some of his past life and the influences that had taken him down the wrong road. We learned that his mother had died in childbirth when Benjo was ten years old. His father, even though he was the teacher in their tiny rural village, was unable to take care of his children, so they were sent to live with relatives.

Benjo moved in with an uncle, a miner in the large silver mines of Potosi. The miners there usually died young because of the harsh working conditions. With another mouth to feed, Benjo's cousins had to give up some of their food, and he grew increasingly uncomfortable with the living arrangements.

As Christmas approached, the cousins told Benjo that the mining officials would give all the miners' children a toy to celebrate Jesus' birthday. Benjo had never had a toy in his entire life. Eagerly he stood in line with his cousins as the mine official handed out the gifts. How thrilled he was when he was given a little truck.

A few minutes later, another mine official went down the list, checking every child's name. When he came to Benjo, the official exclaimed, "Oh, you're not the son of a miner. Here, give that truck back! You shouldn't get a toy!"

Benjo was deeply hurt. In his childish mind, he connected the birthday of Jesus with the toy. When it was taken from him, he supposed that God only sent good things to children who had homes and families. It made him think again that God was the "god of the rich" and that He did not care about poor orphans.

Yet, before she died, Benjo's mother had asked her children to find a church to attend if they ever left their isolated village. Soon after he left his uncle's home to live on the streets of Potosi, Benjo began looking for a church. He found two—one where the congregants burned candles and one where they sang choruses. (That translated for Ken and me into a Catholic church and a Protestant church.)

By this time, Benjo was picking up odd jobs, barely making enough money to stay alive and certainly never enough to take away his hunger pains for an entire day. His clothes, of course, were ragged and dirty when he entered the first church. He was amazed at the luxury of the sanctuary and the elegant dress of the mine officials' wives, who lit candles at the front. As they left the church, one of them held her nose and spoke with disdain, "Go home and take a bath."

So Benjo tried the other church, but the same thing happened. Apparently, these middle-class people did not want a street urchin in Sunday school with their children. Again, the thought that God was for the rich, not for orphans, was re-enforced in his mind.

Others, however, took him in. A group of young people who were actively seeking out the poor and lonely invited him to their meetings, where they gave emotional speeches protesting the ploys of the rich, especially the elite Spanish and the foreign white people who owned and administered the mines. Benjo's lonely soul was ready to hear their words. A born leader, he was soon leading a cell group that searched out other poor youth to join the Trotskyite Communist Party of Bolivia, the most militant and revolutionary party in the country.

When he was in his late teens, Benjo led a march from Potosi to La Paz, protesting the way miners were treated. While rioting in the streets of La Paz, he was approached by the party's leaders, who asked him to go to the Alto Beni and homestead in order to convince the homesteaders to join their party. He readily went along as one of the original seventy settlers of the region.

In those days, fourteen years before our arrival, the road did not go all the way to Sapecho. The newcomers had to walk the last fifty-five miles with everything they owned wrapped in a blanket tied to their backs. What a treasure Benjo was to us, helping us learn the origin of our little village. He was an open book, ready to share with us the early history of Sapecho, for he had been there from the beginning, participating in all aspects of village life.

At that time Ken and I had no idea that God was leading Ken and Benjo together to start CENATEC, a technology center in Bolivia. Later, out of that, SIFAT (Servants in Faith and Technology) in Alabama would be birthed.

Learn and Serve Teams

Many of our friends in churches in the U.S. were interested in our mission in Sapecho. Three young people who had heard us speak and were following our column in the local paper, had written and asked if they could live with us for the summer to help out.

Ken and I felt that God spoke to us from

First John 3:18 long ago, urging us to do more than just use words for Him. "Let us not love with words or tongue, but with actions and in truth." That was one of many Scriptures on which we based our work in Sapecho, and later expanded it into SIFAT.

We realized these young people were hearing this call, too, and decided to invite them to live with us, to learn and to serve. We knew that if they came, the Bolivians would teach them more about serving God than they could ever learn in their traditional environments. So we invited them to join us and called them our Learn and Serve Team. We definitely could use them to work alongside us, but we also wanted this to be an experience that would bring them closer to God and an understanding of the needs of the world that break the heart of Christ.

The day finally dawned for the arrival of these three Learn and Serve summer volunteers. We had sent our fifteen-year-old son Chris to meet their plane in La Paz. It would take him a week to go up the Andes, meet their plane and get them safely back down to the Alto Beni. With no phones in Sapecho, we had learned to be patient.

Early Sunday morning we heard a truck. As

usual, we joined the other villagers hurrying to the road to see who was coming. Chris and four others got off the back of the truck. They unloaded twenty-three duffle bags, suitcases and boxes, and then Chris declared that there was one more. The other passengers in the truck obligingly searched for the missing bag, but it was not to be found. After promising to look for it, the driver left.

At last we could get acquainted with our Learn and Serve Team. There were Joy, Robin, and Steve from Alabama—all three, in their late teens. They had to be full of energy, just to be smiling after the long trip down from La Paz.

And then there was a fourth team member. He was a tall Japanese man, whom Chris introduced as Señor Toshe. We had not expected him. Mr. Toshe was an expert in fish production and had been sent by the Japanese government to help the Bolivian government. Unfortunately, he knew only a few words of Spanish and only a little English. But we were grateful that the Bolivian Ministry of Agriculture had sent him to spend a few days with us to assist with our fish project.

The neighbors came to help us carry in the bags and boxes, and we were amazed at the tools, the Bible School materials and other things sent by churches and friends of the team to help in our work. On the frontier, where even a patch to mend a pair of pants was hard to find, everything they brought was worth much more than its original value. The day after they arrived, Chris went back across the Beni River and recovered the lost package at the bus station.

Our first Learn and Serve Team: Joy Whaley, Robin Warnes and Steve Woodward

The following week was an interesting one, to say the least. Communication was a major undertaking with the diverse groups in our home. There were Steve, Robin and Joy, who spoke English, of course. There were always Spanish-speaking visitors in our house and often Aymarans and Quechuans, with their tribal languages, and then there was Mr. Toshe, who spoke only Japanese. Since Mr. Toshe could not communicate with us beyond a few words, he merely nodded his assent and accompanied us to observe whatever task was at hand. Although we experienced only limited communication with this houseguest from yet another culture, we enjoyed having him with us for a few days.

SIFAT—The Seed Is Planted

This Learn and Serve Team, along with Benjo Paredes, immediately became involved in the work. It was at this point that Benjo and Ken began dreaming of an Institute of Technology that would help the homesteaders survive. Together, they began to look for the right land, where they could experiment to find better ways of producing protein. They were also searching for other methods of using native materials to produce the foods and materials necessary to live in this area.

Although we did not know it at the time, this Institute of Technology, which was later incorporated in Bolivia as CENATEC, (National Center of Appropriate Technology) was the mother of what would become SIFAT, Servants in Faith and Technology. We were unaware that God had positioned us right in the middle of the best possible place to learn community development and the ways in which appropriate technology could help. We had thought that we were coming here to teach the Bolivian people and help them develop their community spiritually and physically, but they were teaching us so much more. The village of Sapecho and the jungle around it became the school where we would learn the things that would empower us to found SIFAT some three years later.

Steve started by building a solar distiller for pure water. We hoped it would produce enough drinking water for a family when they had no pot to boil water in. This particular model was small and only produced a cup a day, but it was successful and the villagers were impressed and began to experiment on their own.

At one point, a man from the government homesteaders' office stopped by to tell Ken that forty new homesteads, just seven miles into the jungle from Sapecho, were laid out and ready to be offered to the public. He suggested that Ken and Benjo accompany him to take a look at the land, hoping that they would consider putting the Institute of Technology there.

The Learn and Serve team and some of the children decided to go along, so early one morning Benjo came to guide them into the jungle, and the group set out to scout a possible site for the Institute. It was an exciting day, but a very tiring one for the explorers, who plunged into an area of the jungle with no paths, hacking their way with machetes as they went.

They didn't return until after dark. Ken told me how impressed he had been with the land. There was a beautiful stream, with its headwaters in the mountains, where it was cool enough for trout; downstream, the water left the woods to flow through a valley, where the temperature was hot enough to grow the tropical fish, tilapia. The explorers came back with tales of mahogany trees so big that one tree would provide the wood for an entire house!

All the way, that long day, they had feared seeing snakes, but did not find a single one. That night, however, as Karen went to the outhouse, her screams alerted the neighborhood. Coiled in a corner of the outhouse was a snake, a boa constrictor. They had not seen one all day in the jungle, only here, in our back yard! Karen was not impressed by the fact that it was only a small one.

◊

As more and more people heard about the work and wanted to serve, one of our immediate tasks was to provide enough room for the visitors. Since there were no motels in Sapecho and since many homesteaders were coming into this area, those passing through were constantly needing a place to spend the night too.

When Elena, the indigenous Methodist teacher of knitting and weaving, came to spend a week with us to give classes in Sapecho, she slept on our dining room table. Better than sleeping on our dirt floor, at least. Steve slept in his pup tent; Robin, on narrow church benches; Joy shared a half-bed with Karen. But these young people had such sweet spirits, they never complained about their meager accommodations.

We also welcomed two teachers, Ann Hood and Miria Gardner from Alabama, who came to teach our children for a month and give them final examinations to see if they had learned enough at home that year to pass their grades. But before they came, we had to make a place for them to sleep. The team, our children and our neighbor, Sato, set out to build a room onto the back of the church for the teachers. He and his helpers spent several days carrying bamboo out of the jungle to build the walls, beds and a "desk" for them.

When Ann and Miria arrived, they accepted their rustic room with warmth and grace, and immediately began to get acquainted with the neighbors as well as tutor our children. They would go to the creek during the hottest part of the day to wash their clothes along with the other Sapecho women. Their smiles and attempts at speaking Spanish endeared them to the whole village. They were settled into their new home just in time for the district women's seminar we were soon to have in the church.

(opposite page)
Sarah (far right), teaching the village women

Chapter Nine

Education: Key to Survival

If we could only read, we would feel like real people," said one of the Aymarans one day. "When we can't read, we feel stupid."

Ken and I had also heard *Hermano* Mauricio's story. The oldest member of the Sapecho Church, this dear man lived next door to us, kept the grass cut around the church and took special care of the church's interests. Many days we could see him sitting in the doorway of his adobe hut, squinting in the early morning sun, sounding out the words in his Bible. More than once he told us, with tears in his eyes, how thankful he was that he had finally learned to read.

"My grandfather was killed after he was found hiding behind the door of the schoolhouse to listen to the reading lessons," *Hermano* Mauricio told us. "The community leaders bound him and called a town meeting to show the rest of us *Indios* (Indians) what would happen if we ever tried anything like that. They tied him to a mule and ran the beast around and around the town plaza, dragging my grandfather and kicking him until he was dead. We *Indios* knew our place back then. We did not dare try to learn to read—not until after the revolution. After that, they said we could legally be *people,* not just *sub-humans* anymore."

Even though Bolivia was about 85 percent indigenous, the country was controlled by the Spanish minority. They knew that the ability to read was a powerful tool that would help free the masses from oppressive working conditions in which they were considered only menial servants and given little pay. Because of the degrading way the leading social class looked at the indigenous, calling them *"Indios"* in the same breath with "stupid, dumb, dog" and any other derogatory term they could think of, the indigenous people often felt that they were ignorant, or else why were they so mistreated and poor?

Unwilling to risk losing their cheap source of labor, the ruling class did not permit indigenous children to attend school before the revolution of 1952. Twenty-five years later, when our family lived there, some villages in rural Bolivia still had no schools. In Sapecho, there was a two-room school where classes were taught through the fourth grade. The homesteaders' children, with only two or three grades, actually had a better education than their parents.

Moved by their plight, Ken and I were determined to do something to help, and the literacy project was born.

The Literacy Project

Taking with us two young adults, Marta and José, who had had the opportunity of eight years of schooling before moving to the Alto Beni, we traveled to Caranavi some seventy-five kilometers away, to attend a three-day workshop offered in the church there. The class was given by Alfalit, a literacy organization that provides materials and uses an effective method for teaching adults to read. With this method, an average Spanish-speaking adult could learn to read in three months, studying only an hour a day for five days a week.

Classes were announced in the three communities where Marta, José and I were to teach. It was the main topic of conversation whenever the women got together. "Are you going to the classes?" they asked each other. Sadly, many of them felt it was a waste of time because they felt in their hearts that they were incapable of learning.

We began to see that even though the people had legal rights, prejudice had robbed them of many social rights, and their own low self-esteem further bound them. Now when schools were opened to them, many believed they probably would not be able to learn. Their political freedom had not freed them from the bondage of centuries of erroneous beliefs handed down from parent to child. They needed first of all to learn to believe in themselves.

A group of about fourteen women came timidly, yet with mounting excitement, to the first class. It was quite a challenge to teach because there were no babysitters, and all of them brought their small children with them. But with the Alfalit method, they were soon reading short sentences.

◊

Asunta, a beautiful, shy Aymaran mother, twenty-eight years of age, was eager to learn. Like so many in the Alto Beni, however, she was hindered by low self-esteem. She bought a Bible and a hymnal and always opened them in the church services, even though she might hold the books upside down, hoping perhaps that something would rub off if she stared hard enough at the pages. I felt sure that she would have been among the first to attend the classes, but she did not come.

Later, when I visited her, she shook her head sadly. "How I wish I could read," she confided in me, "but it is a waste of time. I must learn to live with my disgrace. My dad sent me when the public schools opened for Indians, but I was just too stupid. So he took me out of school to work."

"How long did you attend?" I asked.

"Two whole weeks."

I was shocked that Asunta felt so certain that she could not learn because she had not succeeded in two weeks. No matter what I said to convince her that she could learn, she would not come to our adult literacy classes. Yet she spoke two languages fluently and led the church women's group. I had often heard her give moving extemporaneous speeches. Once she asked me to write my name on a piece of paper and then she wove it into a blanket, perfectly manipulating the thread to form my name, although she did not know a single letter.

But one morning Asunta surprised me at my door before breakfast. *"Hermana!"* she exclaimed with tears in her eyes. "I had the most beautiful dream! I have never dreamed about God before… really, I've been a little afraid of Him because I am so dumb and useless." Her lovely, intelligent face lit up as she continued, "But last night I dreamed that I was sitting in my doorway, and Jesus came over the lemon tree right down to where I was sitting. In my dream, He sat beside me and put His arm around me. *Hermana,* He wasn't mad at me! And He showed me a paper with words on it."

Asunta, with her children Oswaldo, Theodora and Blanquita

Her voice rose in her excitement, and forgetting her usual timidity, she gave me a big hug. *"Hermana,* I read every word on the paper! I wasn't stupid anymore. Jesus showed me how to read!" Then her voice dropped to a whisper. "I want to register for the classes, *Hermana.* I know I can learn. I know Jesus was telling me He will help me."

It was my turn to be afraid because one month of the three-month class had already passed. Joining the group so late might cause Asunta to feel more stupid than ever when she saw how far behind she was. But, no! She was sure that Jesus was going to help her learn to read. Believing in herself and in God gave her the confidence she needed to excel, and soon she had not only caught up but graduated at the head of the class.

Retreat for the *Hermanas*

Many three-day workshops and one-day seminars were offered in the Alto Beni for the men. Government and agency teachers instructed the homesteaders in how to care for farm animals, how to grow chocolate, how to milk and make cheese and other helpful things. Very few seminars had been offered for the women. Some of the young wives and mothers were orphans themselves and had had no one at home to teach them as they grew up.

One reason the women were not often invited to these seminars was that there were no babysitters and most of the women had children. Even the older women with grown children were usually rearing grandchildren or the child of a neighbor who had died in childbirth. Nevertheless, our church decided to offer a week-long seminar for women in the Alto Beni.

Rosita Quispe, president of the Methodist Women in Bolivia, was sent by the national church to lead the event. An Aymaran herself, Rosita was not only able to teach the things she had learned in the university and seminary, but also the ancient native crafts—sewing without a pattern, weaving, knitting, crocheting and spinning thread out of cotton or wool.

Mary Hoey and Rosa Caufield, missionaries from across the river, taught nutrition, cooking and a class in theology. I taught the Bible and parenting for mothers. The church had hired a lady to cook for all those who came, freeing the women to study during the week.

At the end of the rice harvest season, it was customary for the homesteaders to offer a portion of their harvest as a thanksgiving offering to God. This year the church used these offerings to feed the women who came to the school. Several days before the classes were to begin, the Sapecho people began bringing in food. Our back porch was soon filled with bananas, oranges, grapefruit, avocados, rice and chocolate. Mingling with all the other produce were chickens tied to stakes, ready to be killed as needed. One homesteader gave a pig. From the looks of things, the students would not go hungry.

Many women walked miles to get to Sapecho and stayed all week; others came for a day or so at a time. Almost all of them brought from one to four small children. Despite our attempts to provide a nursery and separate classes for the children, the little ones were used to staying at their mother's side or tied to her back and were too frightened to leave her.

On the first day of the seminar, at least seventy-five women and children squeezed into the little Sapecho church. There was such a racket, it was impossible to hear. The cries of the children drowned out the teachers. We had to stop and ask mothers with smaller children to sit near the door and take their children out if they cried. It was a new concept for them, but they adapted well.

At each session, eight or ten women had to be outside with their children, and they usually gravitated toward the corner of the yard where the dinner was being prepared. Some of the women helped the cook while others watched the little ones. That left a fairly quiet audience for the classes.

There were still a number of interruptions. Several babies were sick and others cried for hours at a time. But with all this, the women learned many things. Their ability to concentrate while nursing one baby, with another small child pulling on their skirts, was amazing. They were so eager to learn that they had developed an ability to close out distractions and listen to the lessons.

Each woman learned how to sew, crochet or knit. They all learned how to plan well-balanced meals and were given recipes for new dishes. Some learned to sign their names. They were also taught new concepts from the Bible, and some, for the first time, felt the love of Jesus touch their hearts.

Hunger for Knowledge

After the seminar was over, the women near Sapecho wanted to continue to study at least once a week. We were delighted to accommodate them and offered classes in Bible, literacy for adults who could not read, health, cooking, sewing, music and other subjects.

One of the disadvantages of "civilization" was that it introduced polished rice to the people. When the homesteaders' nutritious whole grain rice was polished, the bran that was flaked off took with it most of the vitamins, leaving mainly carbohydrates. Since most of the rice was automatically polished at the mills, and the bran was fed to the animals, people who were already undernourished received fewer and fewer nutrients.

When we explained this to the women of Sapecho in a course on nutrition, they decided to do something about it. They decided to experiment with the rice bran to see if they could make it palatable. Each Saturday for four weeks, they concocted recipes using the rice bran. The last Saturday they served a meal with every dish containing the bran.

The first course was a tasty soup thickened with rice bran. The entree consisted of rice bran cakes. The bran had been ground and mixed with flour, chopped onions, garlic and other herbs, then formed into patties and fried. Bran was also used to bake bread, cookies, cake, tortillas and turnovers with a fruit filling. For their drink, they boiled rice bran in water with cinnamon and sugar. Delicious! Even though these women lacked formal schooling, they were resourceful, intelligent and eager to learn, and their meal was a highlight of the week.

The Extension Seminary

One of the most successful programs of the Bolivian Methodist Church was the extension seminary. The church trained teachers in basic health, administration and Bible, and sent them out to different villages to hold two-week courses. Twice a year in the capital city, there was a month-long course. Many who did not know how to read went to the seminary. There the teachers began wherever the people were, perhaps teaching them to read, or with more advanced studies when they were ready for them.

This attempt to improve their lot in life and to grow in the knowledge of God did not come without great sacrifice. One of the men who finished a course in the city was eager to share what he had learned with his family and neighbors back home, but had to wait half a day to catch a ride on a supply truck. He rode the rest of the day as far as the truck would take him and spent the night in a village, sleeping on the ground. The next day he continued his journey on foot, walking for two days to his home village far out in the jungle. On his back he was carrying everything he had needed for the month at the seminary—his blanket to wrap up in at night as he slept on the church floor in La Paz; his bowl, cup, and spoon; one change of clothing, his sweater and his Bible. He carried his jug of water in one hand.

Among those attending one month-long seminar in La Paz were two children whose father, a local lay preacher, had felt the need for more theological training. A few months earlier, the children's mother had been returning from selling their bananas in the nearest town and had died in a wreck that occurred when the supply truck in which she was a passenger slid off the road and plunged over the side to the riverbed hundreds of feet below. Having no one to care for his children at home, the father was forced to take them with him to the seminary. They sat quietly through the classes, probably absorbing as much from the lessons as many adults.

One of our local leaders in the Sapecho Church, Crisologo Apaza, was an enthusiastic student of the extension seminary. After the session in La Paz, he returned to teach us all he had learned. Quoting Proverbs 10:14, he said, "Wise men store up knowledge," and then declared, "But how can we store up knowledge if we barely can read and have no books?"

Crisologo walks to a neighboring village to teach what he has learned in the Extension Seminary.

"Before I was a Christian," he continued, "I was like someone living in darkness. But now I feel that God has shone light on us, and this extension seminary is giving us more light. We can't stop learning now. We have a chance to store up knowledge. There is so much more to know!"

Seeing Crisologo, the pastor, and the women come alive with the joy of learning, both spiritually and physically, reminded me of the verse in Isaiah 9:2: "The people walking in darkness have seen a great light; on those living in the land of the shadow of death, a light has dawned."

But it was Asunta, the young Aymaran mother, who taught me one of the most important principles of education and of life itself—the principle that belief in oneself is important to God. It is He who empowers us to learn.

Many of the poor in the Alto Beni had told me that they believed they were poor because they were stupid. God used a dream to break this bondage in Asunta, and He can use us to mirror back to others their own self-worth. When people come to understand their importance to God, it is much easier for them to build upon His promises for a hope-filled future for themselves, their families and their community.

(opposite page)
Ken meets Abdon Paredes, a leader of the Sapecho Church,
in the little town of Puerto Linares where they go for supplies.

Chapter Ten

A *Mobilidad* for the *Hermanos!*

*For I have learned to be content, whatever the circumstances....
I can do all things through Christ who strengthens me.*
—Philippians 4:11, 13

Late one lonely night, I sat in a little bamboo, thatched-roof restaurant on stilts, perched on the banks of the Beni River. That night I was especially thankful that they had some soup left for me. Looking out through the open spaces cut in the walls for windows, I could see across the river the lights of Puerto Linares, reflected in the water. How I would like to be over there, but it was dark and the canoe taxi would not cross again until morning.

As I ate my soup, I recalled the four wonderful days we had just spent with my mother and some dear friends from the States. My dream of being able to share our new home in Bolivia with my parents was partially fulfilled when my mother came for a visit, along with two good friends, Geneva Messer, Hilda Camp and Hilda's ten-year-old son, Ben.

I sat at the small table, recalling the events as they had unfolded....

◊

Ken had been in La Paz, working through all the government red tape required before he could pick up the new jeep which the people in Alabama had just bought for the church in the Alto Beni. While he was there, Bob Caufield received a radio message from the States, saying that my mother and friends were arriving in La Paz on Wednesday. It was Tuesday when I got the message in Sapecho. What a surprise! How excited I was when I heard they were coming! There was no way I could get up the mountain to meet them on such short notice, but we got a radio message through to Ken in La Paz to meet their plane.

Typical of the way things happen in Bolivia, my mother and friends had to wait four days in La Paz before they could get a bus down to the Alto Beni. Since they only had two weeks total time, including travel to and from Sapecho, the prospects for a substantial visit seemed dim. Resigned to the inevitable, however, I waited eagerly for Saturday night.

When they arrived in Sapecho, we realized that by the time they traveled back to La Paz to board the plane for the States, they would have only four days with us. That was most frustrating because I needed at least three or four weeks to share with them just the highlights of the Alto Beni. But there seemed to be no solution except to be thankful for the time we did have. I planned to prolong the visit by accompanying them back to La Paz and at least see them off at the airport.

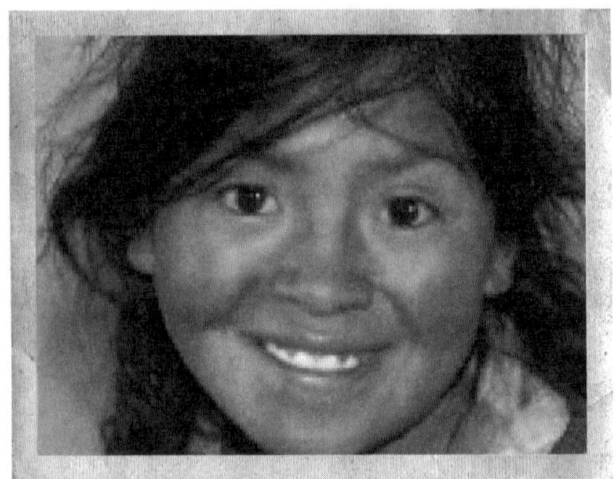

One of the little children in the Alto Beni

Lost!

It was too bad that Ken had not yet been able to bring the jeep, because on the fourth day of their visit in Sapecho with us....we spent all afternoon waiting for a *mobilidad* to hitch a ride to the Caufields's so that we would be ready to catch the bus to La Paz at daybreak the next morning. As night approached and still no truck had passed, I began to fear that we would not be able to get out. That would mean our guests would be stranded in Sapecho for four more days until the next bus came down, which meant that they would miss their plane back to Alabama.

I remembered that in the chocolate experiment station, sometimes a man with a pickup spent the night, so I left the others waiting with their baggage on the side of the road while I walked the mile to the station. Maybe we could hire the man to take us to the river. But he was not there, so our last hope of transportation dwindled.

I walked hurriedly to get back to the others before dark, but someone else was walking behind me even faster. At the creek, Señora Ramirez caught up with me. "Oh, *Hermana!*" she called out to me in a voice trembling with fear. "My daughter is gone! We left the two children in the house while my husband and I were harvesting *cacao*. When we got home, eight-year-old Sandra was gone and is nowhere to be found! Our four-year-old is hysterical. She says Sandra walked off into the grove of chocolate trees and disappeared. Oh, *Hermana,* I'm so afraid she was bitten by a snake! I know she'd be home before dark if something hadn't happened."

We hurried on toward Sapecho. None of my family or visitors were by the roadside where I had left them. In the nearby *pensión* (native restaurant), they told me Tommy had stopped a jeep going the other way and had spent fifteen minutes talking the man into turning around and taking them back to the river so they wouldn't lose the tickets on the bus and plane.

I was glad that they had found a *mobilidad,* but I feared it would be too late for them to get across the river to the Caufields. That would mean they'd have to sleep on a straw mat on a floor if they were lucky enough to get someone to share their roof. But at least they would be at the river, ready to cross by daylight, and could catch the bus.

Still, I felt a great disappointment descending upon me. I had not been able to meet them when they arrived, and now I wouldn't be able to reach them in time to accompany them to the airport so we could spend some more precious hours together. I had not even told them goodbye!

I stood there a moment, trying to swallow the lump in my throat, when I suddenly became aware of Señora Ramirez weeping beside me. She had hunted the town over, and everywhere she had turned, she had met with the same response: No one had seen Sandra in Sapecho that afternoon. That meant she had to be somewhere on their farm, in the chocolate grove or in the jungle. It was time to forget my own disappointment and get busy helping to look for the lost child.

After returning home for a flashlight, we

hurried back to her hut about a kilometer away. Joining her distraught husband, we spread out through the chocolate grove, calling and searching for Sandra.

And then I heard a truck coming in the distance—how strange that a vehicle would be passing at this time of night. Maybe I could catch a ride and get to the river to join my mother and my friends in time to make the bus to La Paz, after all. At least I could tell them good-bye....

I was in the chocolate grove near the road when I saw the lights of the truck approaching. It had been a long time since I had wanted anything as badly as I wanted to catch that truck...but I knew I could not leave those parents alone. A few months ago their little son had died, and I was almost convinced that little Sandra had joined him. Neither the jungle nor the chocolate grove was a safe place for a child at night. How could I leave them now? I knew I could not.

Aching all over with longing, I stood near the road and quietly watched the truck drive by without me. *Good-bye, Mother! Good-bye Hilda! Good-bye, Geneva! Good-bye, Ben!* I cried silently across those miles to the river. *At least we had four days,* I tried to reassure myself as I returned to the search for little Sandra.

The truck had not been gone five minutes when we found her asleep under a chocolate tree, all safe and sound. We took her home and I said good-night, walking the dark road back to Sapecho with a lonely heart.

To keep back my tears, I kept thanking God for the four days I had spent with loved ones from home. But when I got to Sapecho, I heard an incredible sound. It was another *mobilidad!* When trucks were so scarce, especially at night, could another one really be coming? Suddenly my loneliness dissipated. My heart was singing as I climbed up on top of the big truck loaded with bags of rice.

The load was so heavy that the truck must have averaged no more than ten miles an hour, but I didn't care. We bumped over those ten miles to the river for almost two hours, but it was the nicest ride I had had in a long time.

Blessings on Top of Blessings!

When we got to Santa Ana, the little community on the river bank across from Puerto Linares, I found that my folks had arrived in time to cross over. Surely they were safe with the Caufields on the other side. But I could not reach them as no canoe taxis crossed the river at night. So near, but still so far.

I found a place where they would lend me a straw mat and a corner of the floor and then went into the little restaurant for a bowl of soup. Would I be able to get a canoe early in the morning before the bus left with my mother and friends? Puerto Linares seemed so close, just across the river. Yes, the kerosene lights in the homes and shops were beautiful, reflecting in the water, but that river had the final word...unless God spoke differently. It divided me from my loved ones just as surely as if we were a hundred miles apart.

Then, all of a sudden, Steve Caufield, the missionaries' sixteen-year-old son, came walking in. "Steve! What are you doing on this side of the river?" I greeted him. "It's too late for you to get across and go home tonight. What brings you here?"

"I came for you, Aunt Sarah," he replied. (Missionary children usually call other missionaries Aunt and Uncle.) As he spoke, an indigenous boy came in and stood beside him, a boat oar in his hand. "My friend Lucho here has a dugout canoe. We got permission from the Navy to cross at night and bring you over."

I kept thinking that this must surely be a dream until we were in the dugout and Steve and Lucho were rowing upstream in the shallow edge of the river. After we were some distance above the lights of Puerto Linares, they moved the canoe out into the mainstream and rowed hard to get across before the current took us below Puerto Linares. On the other side was Rosa Caufield, Steve's mother, with a flashlight to help us make our way through the huge piles of green bananas which had been unloaded on the shore.

People were sleeping on blankets on the ground near their bananas, waiting for the dawn and hoping for a truck to take their produce to market in La Paz. I stepped over the sleeping people, picked my way through the piles of bananas, and gratefully climbed into the Caufields's jeep to go to their home where Mother and my friends waited.

◊

The next morning Rosa got up at five o'clock to fix breakfast for us and help us to get off. There were eight of us: Mother; Hilda; Geneva; Ben; Ann Hood, the teacher who had been with us a month; Tommy, Karen and I.

The trip up the mountain on Death Road was a memorable experience. Our family had become accustomed to the hair-raising sharp curves and sheer precipices, but our guests were in shock as we rode the bus to La Paz. Part of the way, Hilda was sitting on the floor in the aisle, her eyes clenched shut, not daring to look out the window.

A splash of local color was added by the pig that one man was taking to La Paz. The pig wouldn't stay under the man's seat even though he was tied by a string. In his attempt to escape, the pig kept rubbing against Geneva's leg. The man seated behind us held a straw bag full of baby chickens which kept sliding down under our feet.

Our neighbor, Cristina, and her new husband were on the same bus with us. Two months ago I had participated in their wedding in an indigenous ceremony. Her husband, Costo, had been married before and had lost his first wife a year before in childbirth.

Since he could not work and take care of his newborn baby, he had put her in a children's home. Now that he had married Cristina, he was coming to La Paz to get his child from the home and take her to live with them. He was one happy man. *"Hermana,"* he told me, "now I can have a wife and my baby too. God has been so good to me!"

He went on to explain that the orphanage would not allow him to take his child unless he had a house in La Paz. The little shack on his farm in the Alto Beni was not allowed by the officials of the children's home, for they had no way of knowing whether it existed or not. So he was coming to La Paz to build in order to regain custody of his baby.

Costo had very little money, but he had planted a watermelon crop. Watermelons, like rice and chocolate, are a money crop in Bolivia. He needed $50 to build the little one-room house to satisfy the director of the orphanage. Robin Warnes, one of the Learn and Serve Team who had decided to stay on with us for a year, loaned him the money from the amount she had set aside for her return trip. Costo planned to repay her with proceeds from the sale of his melons.

When we got off the bus in La Paz, Cristina and Costo got off with us. Pointing to a church high up the sides of the rim surrounding La Paz, Costo explained, "A block beyond that is where we'll be building our home. Since you have four days in La Paz, couldn't you come visit us before you leave?"

We agreed to try, and as we told them good-bye, Cristina shyly handed us a spindle with some cotton she had been spinning into thread. "Your mother and your friends enjoyed watching me make thread from cotton," she said. "So I wanted to give them my spindle to remember me by. Maybe they can take it to the United States and learn to make their own thread." Cristina was an Aymaran who knew all the crafts of her ancestors. She made thread of cotton or wool, dyed it, and wove beautiful blankets.

When they left, I went into the bus station to call Ken. He had been in La Paz a month, each day filling in papers and standing in lines in the customs building, trying to get the jeep. It was great to hear his voice on the phone, and the news he gave me was more cause for rejoicing. "Sarah!" he told me excitedly. "I have the *mobilidad!* I have the jeep!" The long-awaited day had arrived.

The children, our visitors and I waited at the bus station until Ken came to take us to the church's hospitality center where we would stay the four more days until their plane left for Alabama.

At least we would have that extra time with Mother and our friends.

Tom and Ken, in front of the new *mobilidad*

When Ken drove up, he was in a new Toyota 4-wheel-drive, long-bed pickup with a removable canvas that converted the whole truck into a jeep. All the hours and days we had spent walking to and from our services or waiting on the side of the road, hoping for a passing truck, were in the past now. All the frustration of trying to get sick people to a doctor when there was no *mobilidad*, was only a memory. In our hands was a beautiful vehicle, ready to be used to serve God and humanity. My heart cried out thanks to Him and to the churches in North Alabama who had made this moment a reality.

Palos Blancos

Palos Blancos was a busy, dusty little town on Sundays. The homesteaders from miles around came in to play soccer and socialize with their neighbors. The few local stores, where one could buy most of the necessities of life, were open on those days.

When the road was passable, several dozen more businessmen and women came down from La Paz with big bundles of merchandise tied in blankets on their backs. The peddlers could be found crowding the sides of the road in the middle of town, their colorful blankets spread out on the ground, their merchandise arranged over the blankets. Often there was a piece of plastic or cloth stretched, umbrella fashion, over a frame on a post to shade these street merchants and their wares from the torrid sun or to protect them from the rain.

Every Sunday morning about eight o'clock, I passed down the four blocks of streets to the crossroads of Palos Blancos, greeting the peddlers, then went on a block farther down the dusty road to the little church where I was the pastor.

At least twenty-five or thirty children were

always waiting for Sunday school, after which the adults would join them. The men always came first, leaving their wives to prepare dinner. Halfway through the service, the women would appear. They encouraged me to extend the teaching so they could hear some of it, too.

At 12:30 or 1:00, the people were dismissed to go home and eat. After only a half-hour or so, they were back, ready for more—a class in literacy, a Bible class, nutrition and music, which was like a choir practice where they learned new hymns. I would also do my best to teach anything else they were interested in.

Once they asked for a geography class to help them picture the world beyond their borders. Although they were most intelligent and taught me much about their own environment, they were isolated in their jungle communities, with few resources for learning things outside of their daily experience. No one had television, of course, and very few had radios.

About four or five o'clock, we would end the classes and I would start the seven-mile walk home. Before the jeep arrived, it took two and a half hours to reach Sapecho on foot. Only if a supply truck passed would I be able to hitch a ride and get home any earlier.

One Sunday, Don Luis came on his bicycle from a little village some distance farther into the jungle. This was the fifth time he had come to ask for someone from the Palos Blancos church to come teach the Word of God in his village.

We had not been able to respond because it was too far to walk there and back in one day, but this week, we had *mobilidad,* the new jeep! After our Sunday school and church services, the people went home to eat a quick lunch, and returned to *ride* to our first service in Don Luis's village. When I came back from my meal with one of the church members, the jeep was almost full of the *hermanos.*

"Where are your wives?" I asked.

"Wives never go anywhere," one of them replied. "They want to stay home and cook."

"Did you ask them?"

"Well, no," another responded, "but I'm sure my wife wouldn't want to go. She likes to work in her kitchen."

"I'd feel better if your wives went with us. Would you please just ask them?"

They looked at each other in surprise. "Do you really suppose our wives might like to go?" they asked each other. "Let's go ask them!"

Evidently the wives *did* want to go, for they came running immediately and packed the jeep—so many of them, in fact, that the long-bed Land Rover jeep, made to hold thirteen passengers, accommodated twenty-seven that day! No one minded being crowded. They were as proud of the jeep as we were. It belonged to them as well as to us, because it was a donation from churches in Alabama to the church in the Alto Beni.

We sang choruses as we bumped along the dusty road until we arrived in the new village. Most of the recently settled homesteading communities had no church or trained religious leader.

A dusty circle of about ten thatched-roof houses, the little town had been settled on the bank of the big river. As was typical in the jungle, two or three of the houses had turned their front rooms into small stores.

The house where we had been invited to start the new mission was located on a farm near the village. We gathered in the main room of the humble, dirt-floored home where the host had prepared benches that lined the walls. About twenty of us crowded into the little house, while the others stood outside, looking in through the open door and the cracks in the bamboo. We sang hymns, prayed and then different *hermanos* gave their testimonies of experiences in which God had helped them. Afterward, I taught a Bible lesson.

Then the homeowner spoke, thanking us for coming and explaining how they had wanted to learn more about God for a long time. He asked us if we would return and hold services on a regular basis, using his home as the gathering place.

For the first time in the eleven months we had been in Bolivia, we could say yes! We could come back, because we had the jeep to bring us here. Packed in as we were, all the way home, we sang praises to God for this answer to our prayers.

224

(opposite page)
Sarah, reaching out to the people of the Alto Beni

Chapter Eleven

Healing Hands

A little while without food, I can live.
But it breaks my heart to know I can not give.
I cannot bear to hear sick children cry.
—Kagawa, poet of Japan

With all of the health problems in the Alto
Beni—malnutrition, parasites, tuberculosis and
other ailments—Ken and I often wished we had
studied medicine. We had been deeply affected by
so many children's deaths. About all we could offer
was our pink bottle of Pepto Bismol, some iron
pills and lots of prayer. What we hadn't considered

was the large number of mouth and gum diseases also prevalent in this area.

Some of the people had never seen a dentist before. In this area where food was often scarce, hard candies were the cheapest item one could buy in the little store. No toothbrushes were sold since most people needed to spend their few *pesos* on food. For those who are used to having a dentist available, it would be hard to imagine the condition of the teeth of some of the people.

This week a team of dentists from Alabama were visiting us. Since we had the jeep, we took them about twenty miles farther inland, left the jeep on the bank of the Big River and crossed by dugout canoe.

Walking two miles through the rain forest, we came to a village called San Antonio. Numerous times before, the people here had invited us to come for a service, but this was the first time we had been able to get there. The dental team set up their office in the little schoolhouse, and the people began to arrive. All day the dentists worked, with many still waiting. When night closed in around us, the line of hopeful, hurting people was still long.

"If I had a lamp, I could work on into the night," the dentist told me. But no one in San

Antonio even had a kerosene lamp or lantern. One of the team members held his flashlight for the dentist until the batteries got too dim to see the teeth.

"Tomorrow we'll be in Palos Blancos ten miles from here," we told them. "If your teeth are hurting really badly, you can go there and maybe we can get to you tomorrow."

◊

We walked down the trail under the stars until we saw the river in front of us, flowing by, silently but swiftly. A lone canoe was pulled up against the bank, the owner half asleep. He agreed to row us across for 15 cents each. Three times the canoe crossed to take us and all the dental tools and supplies.

Each time, the indigenous man who owned the canoe rowed upstream along the edge of the river where the current was not swift. When we were some distance above the place we wanted to land, he guided the canoe out into the mainstream, rowing hard to pull us across before we were swept too far downstream.

One *hermana* from Sapecho who had

accompanied us had brought her small son with her. He started to cry as the force of the current hit the side of the canoe and began to rock us from side to side. "Be quiet! Just hold on!" his mother commanded.

We all knelt in the middle of the canoe, clinging to the sides, with the water lapping up on our fingers. The small boy's cries stopped, and we heard only the sound of the oars as they pierced the water again and again, faster and faster, as our oarsman tried to overcome the current.

It was a beautiful, black, starry night. Millions of diamonds sparkled overhead. No one spoke as our skilled guide brought the canoe alongside another canoe tied up on the shore. Here a path led to the place where our jeep was parked. Again the small boy's sharp cry broke the beauty of the night and jolted me back to more practical things as the canoes slid together. His fingers had been pinched between them, but fortunately not badly.

After loading the jeep, we set out in the night over the bumpy, one-lane road, almost too tired to talk. Then Marcelino, one of the newly converted young people from Sapecho, picked up the guitar and began to sing. It's amazing how music can renew our strength. Soon we all found ourselves singing with gusto as we bumped along in the night.

I think I've never known a greater joy than we felt after spending a day and half the night with these people, trying to serve in some small way in the Spirit of Jesus. That night we were so exhausted we had nothing left in us "except the will which said to us, *Keep on!*" as Rudyard Kipling wrote. At such times the fellowship of what it means to follow Jesus just envelops and strengthens us and makes the commonplace, daily grind of life become a real adventure. We all felt that fellowship as we sang our way home.

We started out again at daybreak, having had little sleep. This time the dentists would be pulling teeth in Palos Blancos. All day long as we translated for them, we saw mouths full of broken, rotted-out teeth, with the stubs still in the gums. We smiled at the patients as we cringed inwardly.

Some of the people in Palos Blancos had brought lanterns with them so that the dentists could work after dark. It was after midnight before they finished with their last patient.

Just as we were ready to pack up to go home, a teenage girl came in. "I just heard a dentist was here," she said. "Please, will you pull my tooth?"

"We cannot accept any more patients," I tried to explain.

Tears welled up in her beautiful brown eyes, already at an early age showing signs of suffering. "You are young," I said. "You could catch a ride to another town, farther out, where there's a dentist."

She shook her head. "I've begged my mother," she answered, "but she said, 'No. We don't have money for a dentist. Pain is part of life. You'll just have to learn to bear it till your tooth rots out.'"

I looked in her mouth, barely able to suppress the repulsion I felt. Her jaw tooth was so rotten, I could hardly stand to look at it. "I'll ask the dentists," I weakened. Neither could they deny her. Past midnight, they continued to pull teeth and treat suffering people.

◊

The next morning back in Sapecho, a group of five men knocked at our door, very politely, very formally. They had walked twenty miles to reach us. "We are a delegation from San Antonio," the leader told me. "Remember us, from the village where you were two days ago? The town had a community meeting after you left and sent us to ask the dentists if they would come and live with us."

He gave an eloquent presentation of the great need of the people of his village for a dentist and doctor. He told how many children cried at night from toothache. Alas for them and for us all, as civilization comes in, it seems to bring candies and soft drinks first of all. But when he finished his plea, I had to tell him the dentist had to leave tomorrow to return to the United States.

"Then only one week," they pleaded. "Will they live with us at least one week? We need them so!"

Oh, how I ached for the people of San Antonio (and for the people of Brecha F, who came with a similar plea a few minutes later.) How I ache for the people of Palos Blancos and of Sapecho and of all the Alto Beni! "No, not even one week," we had to say. "Tomorrow they must go back."

The dentists promised to ask other medical personnel to come share part of their lives with the people of the Alto Beni. So the delegation went home, hoping maybe someone else would come, too. How long can hope endure, smashed between the harsh realities of their lives, like the fingers of that small boy smashed between the canoes on the river?

Is There No Help for Flora?

We had thought the rainy season would be ending, so we helped plan a three-day district retreat for all the churches in the Alto Beni, to be held in the high school near the Caufields. Leaders from the national church in La Paz would speak at the sessions. We could use the school's dining hall, and participants could sleep on straw mats on the floor of the classrooms.

But when the week of the retreat came, it was still raining. It rained all night before the day of the retreat. Yet early that morning, people began to arrive in Sapecho from the outlying farms. They had walked in the rain and were ready for us to leave for the Caufields's place some twelve miles down a muddy road and across the big river.

We took as many as we could pack into our jeep—twenty-four people with their bundles of clothing and their blankets to wrap up in at night—and started out by mid-afternoon, planning to arrive in time for the first service that night.

We had gone only about ten yards when someone in the back of the jeep yelled for us to stop. Looking back, we saw the new *hermana* who had been converted recently, running down the trail toward us, with her baby tied to her back and her two small boys running behind her.

"Oh, can't I go, too?" she cried. "I was here the first thing this morning, but I didn't know we should take blankets. So when someone told me, I went back home to get them. Is there no room for me now?"

I knew it had taken Flora an hour and a half to walk back to her home for the blankets, then another hour and a half to return. Three hours she had been walking rapidly with her baby on her back, leading her two young sons. Her face was red from exertion. Beads of perspiration stood out on her forehead. But the jeep was crammed full; it appeared impossible to make any more room for her family. Disappointment was written all over her face.

"Go ahead, *Hermanos,*" she said sadly. "I see there's no more room. I'll spend the night in the church here and maybe I can get a ride out tomorrow. I need to go so much. I know so little of the Word of God. Surely at this retreat, we'll learn much. Maybe I'll make it in the morning."

We knew something of this woman's hunger for more knowledge of God. How could we go off and leave her? "We'll make room," one sister decided and the others agreed. The long-bed jeep was only built to carry thirteen passengers. Now with twenty-four inside, it wasn't easy to find space for *Hermana* Flora and her three children. But somehow they got in.

It took us three and a half hours to travel the ten miles to the river. Several times I wanted to give up and go back. Once, I was ready to abandon the jeep after a close call when we slid across the muddy road, stopping only inches from a steep drop-off. Twice, the ruts were so deep that the axles dragged, leaving all four wheels spinning in the air. But the enthusiasm of the *hermanos* kept us going. We had no shovel with us to dig out the middle, so the *hermanos* got out of the jeep and used their bare hands.

We had had a real revival in Sapecho without planning it at this particular time. Most of those with us were new Christians. "We're going to make it, Pastor," they kept reassuring us. "All of us need so much to know more of God, and the leaders of the church in La Paz are going to be there to teach us. We can make it through this mud!"

It was almost nightfall when we reached the river, so we didn't expect the ferry to take us across. The captain agreed, however, if we'd take the battery out of the jeep and allow him to borrow it since the ferry was minus a battery today. In the spirit of cooperation, we were soon crossing the river, on our way to the school near the Caufields.

We were not the only ones to arrive late. Parts of the road to La Paz had been destroyed by rains again, Rosa Caufield told us. The ministers who were to conduct the retreat could not get through. Quickly, we would have to plan the retreat ourselves, even now, as it was time to begin.

Exhausted from the tension of the trip, plus suddenly learning that I must shoulder responsibility for some of the long-awaited retreat with no time to prepare, I felt I wouldn't notice the hard floor we slept on that night. I could have slept on a pile of rocks.

But, no! *Hermana* Flora and her three children were lying beside me when she began to cough. Suddenly she jumped up and stumbled over the others who were sleeping, in her haste to get to the door. I heard her gagging and discovered she was vomiting blood.

She came back and lay down at my side. "Pray for me, Sister," she said. "I have tuberculosis. I've been going for treatment for six months now, but I just get worse." A fit of coughing stopped her, and she had to rush to the door again.

I had not known *Hermana* Flora was so sick. That night she didn't sleep at all, coughing and spitting up blood. When morning came, I took her to the nearby clinic. They sent her on to Caranavi, trying to save her life.

Though I returned to the school for the rest of the retreat, I could not forget *Hermana* Flora's brave struggle to get to the meeting, as sick as she was. And she was only able to attend one service, yet she never complained.

Almost a month went by before she was well enough to return to Sapecho. "I'm sorry you missed the rest of the retreat," I told her when I saw her again.

"But I got to be there *one* night," she replied with a smile. "I learned a little more about God."

As soon as she returned home from the

hospital, *Hermana* Flora continued working under the tropical sun, helping her husband harvest the rice. She worked all day, every day, with her baby tied on her back. How could she be healed of tuberculosis this way? But if she didn't help save the rice during the harvest time, there would not be enough for them to eat all year.

Something akin to desperation settles over me as I recall sharing the lives of these hard-working, long-suffering people. In the depths of my being, I know that it is not God's will for some of us to have so much while others face hunger, disease and death daily. And with Kagawa, the poet of the slums of Japan, my heart cries out, "Is there no way that help can come?"

"Do You Have Any Medicine That Can Make Our Children Talk?"

As was so often the case, a man came to our door one day, gravely concerned about his three small children—ages two and three. Although two of them were two years old, they were not twins. One of them belonged to a neighbor who had died in childbirth, so his wife, who was also nursing a baby, took the orphaned child and was rearing her as their own. This man was asking, "Do you have any medicine that will make my children talk?"

Once again I had to shake my head sadly, but promised to seek medical advice for him. I learned that Dr. Crespo, one of the church doctors in Bolivia, would be coming to the Alto Beni and would be in Sapecho the following Wednesday. So two of our volunteers went with me early the next morning to give this man the good news.

We were warmly greeted when we finally arrived at our destination five miles up the mountain behind our village. While we rested from our long walk, the grateful father brought us a hundred-pound sack of oranges and grapefruit from their orchard. We ate several, which helped our dry, parched throats.

Then the couple brought out their children. They were beautiful in appearance, but the way they looked at us gave us the impression that they were retarded. The three little ones sat there listlessly, barely moving. It seemed it was an effort for them to keep their eyes open. Since all three of them were affected—and because one of them was adopted—we suspected that their problem was dietary, perhaps lack of protein.

When we told the parents that the doctor would be in Sapecho the next week, the father replied, "Then we'll go down and sleep in Sapecho on Tuesday night to be sure to be there on time." How this couple loved their children!

There was not much conversation on the way home as we trudged back down the mountain. Our thoughts swirled with the faces of the three small children with their dull, tired eyes. No doubt they were retarded. Was it because of their diet? Had the process gone too far to be reversible? We were no doctors, but the diagnosis seemed likely.

The next week, when Dr. Crespo saw the children, he confirmed our fears. "There is no medicine in this world that can make these children talk," he told us. "They are severely anemic and need protein, iron and vitamins."

He felt that it was too late. The damage was done. Not even our iron pills could help now. Of course we helped with vitamins and teaching them nutrition such as how beans added to their rice would make a protein. One of those children died, but it was Divine Power greater than we who saved two of them.

From Lice to Liberty in Christ

We continued to give what little we had to offer in the hope of alleviating some of the suffering, and God took our "little" and multiplied it.

One morning a teenage boy stood back away from my front door, until I noticed him. Then respectfully, he said, "Good morning, *Señora*." I recognized him as being the boy who had asked permission to build a shelter in which to live on the side of the fish ponds. He would be working in the lot near us, making bricks. Ken had told me that his parents were dead and that he was taking care of his younger brother and sister.

"Come in," I said, and motioned him to a chair at the table. I sat down near him to get acquainted. "You are Florencio, aren't you?"

"Si, *Señora*," he answered hesitantly and after a lengthy pause, stated the purpose of his visit. "I'm worried about my kids, *Señora*," he said. "They have lice in their hair. Do you have any medicine that could kill lice? I need to buy some, but there's none available in Sapecho."

Someone in Alabama had given us a medicated shampoo, so I went with Florencio across the ponds to help him treat his seven-year-old brother and his ten-year-old sister.

His "house" was built of a few pieces of metal roofing, with the ground for a floor and tall grasses tied together for walls. Inside, he had driven a post into the ground and tied saplings to it from two walls, making a platform that filled a corner of the room. Over this he had spread a blanket for a bed for the three of them.

I noticed three bowls, three spoons and three cups on the dirt floor in a corner of the room, along with a blackened cooking pot. On the opposite wall, a big bunch of cooking bananas lay by a basket of grapefruit. A bamboo cane that extended from wall to wall overhead held a few clothes.

It was a home that spoke silently and sharply of poverty, yet it contained all the necessary items for survival. Hanging by a vine wrapped around the bamboo cane, was a nice suitcase of cowhide, like those I had seen in other cities of Bolivia. The suitcase was a clue that these children had once lived in better circumstances.

Little by little, as we became better acquainted with Florencio, his sister Juanita and his little brother Lucio, we learned their story. His father had been a prosperous farmer in another section of Bolivia. They had many fruit trees, sheep and cattle. But by the time Florencio was twelve years old, both his parents were dead. Relatives began to fight over his father's property.

At that early age, Florencio assumed the responsibilities of head of the home. He worked the fields as he had helped his father do before. But when his harvest was ready, relatives stopped by and demanded a percentage of his harvest. They took so much that he didn't have enough to feed little Lucio, Juanita and himself. Florencio was hurt with all the arguing and fussing and found no peace among his own people in his own town. So he packed the bare essentials in his father's good suitcase, took his brother and sister and started out across Bolivia to find a place where he could live in peace.

For five years Florencio had wandered over the country, working at any job that presented itself. Being a hard worker, he found that he could make enough to feed his little family, even though he was only a boy. At last he heard about the Alto Beni, where one could homestead his own farm.

From the beginning we had been impressed with Florencio's willingness to work. Every morning when we got up in the first light of dawn, we looked across the fish ponds and saw all three of the children, already busy carrying water or mixing the mud to make more bricks.

We invited them to Sunday school and church, and they came. One day about three weeks after they had moved into the little hut on our ponds, Florencio stood at my door again. He came in and sat down at the table as before.

"Señora," he said again, in a serious tone. "There is something else I need that I cannot buy in Sapecho. I wonder if you could help me this time? I am ashamed to tell you, *Señora,* but I don't have a Bible. We never went to church before we came here. I still don't know much about God since I've only been to church three times, but I feel that I've been raising my kids just like animals. I need a Bible to find out more about God and to teach my kids. Do you have a Bible to sell?"

We found a Spanish Bible. One of our church leaders, Crisologo Apaza, came in while we were talking. He showed Florencio the different books of the Bible and the boy soaked up every word. As Crisologo and I talked with him, explaining the message of Jesus, tears began to run down this strong, independent seventeen-year-old's face. He brushed the tears off and said in a choked voice, struggling to control his emotions, "When I was younger, I thought of God a lot. But then I had a lot of trouble and got so upset inside with all the arguing and fighting, I just forgot about God. That's why I gave my uncles the farm and left. I wanted to find peace. But I've never really found it. I've really never known how to give my life to God. That's why I want a Bible."

Sitting at our table that afternoon, Florencio committed his life to Jesus Christ. Tears ran down his cheeks as he said, "The peace I have been seeking is not found in our surroundings, is it? God gives it to us inside, in spite of our outside problems."

Several weeks later, Florencio was elected secretary of the church's youth group for the whole Alto Beni District. Afterward, he came to us a little shaken. "Please, will you help me?" he pleaded. "I don't know much yet. I'm just beginning." But with such a beginning, there is a good possibility of a great ending.

Orphan Child Becomes "Mother"

After a week in La Paz, we came home to Sapecho to find little ten-year-old Juanita taking care of a child who looked to be less than two years old. When we asked her who he was, she replied, "We don't know. His parents came through Sapecho, walking in the rain, and asked if they could spend the night in the church building. They were sick and coughing so hard they could hardly breathe. They said they were trying to get to some relatives' homestead farther into the jungle. We gave them some rice to eat and lent them a dry blanket, but the next morning they were lying there, dead in the church."

"Does anyone know who their relatives are?"

Juanita, age 10, with her "adopted" orphan child

"No, *Hermana*, we didn't ask their names. No one has ever seen them before. This little boy is too young to tell us anything. The *hermanos* came together to bury the mother and father and then tried to decide who would take the child to raise him. But no one had any extra food for another person," she continued. "They were afraid they might not be able to take care of their own children if they added another mouth to feed. But me and Florencio and Lucio don't have kids. Florencio decided he could get enough food to feed him. So I offered to raise him."

They were really just "kids" themselves. Now, together, the three orphan children decided that it was their responsibility to take in this other little orphan child. "The *hermanos* helped us get a few more clothes for the little boy," Juanita explained. "And they told us they would share their food when they had any extra. We can make it fine. We have a big family here in the church to help out."

This was not the only family in the Alto Beni where children were raising children when their parents died.

Our little family in Sapecho

Generational Servants of God

Because the tragedies all around us affected our children, too, God gave us extra strength to remain calm for their sakes. Although we often felt like giving in to the desperation of our struggling neighbors, we all learned together to do all we could to help, and to leave the rest to God. It was the grace of God that empowered us to face situations we would never have thought we could overcome. One of most special blessings was our experience watching our children grow in their faith and service to the church and to the villagers in our community that we had come to serve.

Kathy served as the village nurse.

Ken and I had no medical training, of course, but our twelve-year-old Kathy was intrigued with the many things she could teach people that would help them stay healthy and, with her compassionate heart, was soon involved in helping the sick. Not a doctor or nurse passed through that she didn't question about ways to bring some measure of comfort to hurting people. One doctor even gave her a stethoscope and blood pressure cuff, and Kathy had a *Physicians' Desk Reference* to look up medicines and find the correct dosages for people of different ages and weights. The women in the village called her *doctorcita* and often sought her out, knowing she would at least listen and sympathize with their ailments, then dispense vitamins or basic first aid.

Karen, caring for the children of our *hermanas*

Ten-year-old Karen helped prepare her friends' baby brothers' or sisters' little bodies for burial. With no funeral homes in the jungle, family or friends took care of building the caskets and dressing the bodies of the dead for the last time. When a death occurred in the family of one of her friends, Karen was always right there to help.

Chris and Benjo, traveling through the Andes

Fifteen-year-old Chris was our errand boy. When it was necessary to go in to La Paz, he often went for us because he had learned to hitchhike over the Andes and could find his way around the capital city much better than we. Going up Death Road on one such trip, Chris and his traveling companions came upon a truck that had just gone over the side of the road and plummeted several hundred feet below. Chris joined the other men and climbed over the precipice to see if anyone was alive. They found only dead bodies, and Chris also helped retrieve them, tying the bodies to ropes so that others could pull them back up to the road, where relatives could come to claim their remains.

During our time in Bolivia, each of our children had learned specific things they could do to help. Eleven-year-old Tommy volunteered for the job of giving the village children some powdered milk each day. With so few cows in the area—only three—milk was scarce, of course. Tommy couldn't give the children milk to drink, because we couldn't keep enough of the polluted water boiled for all of them, but he learned to offer them a little milk powder in a dish to eat with a spoon.

One of Tommy's little friends in Sapecho

Little Margarita, a five-year-old neighbor child, was Tommy's special "student." She came one day asking for Tommy when I was at home. "May I have some milk?" she asked him. "Are my hands clean enough, Tommy? Is my face clean?"

Tommy gave her a little hug and explained to me how he was trying to teach the children to go to the little stream and wash their face and hands every time they got dirty during the day. The powdered milk was their reward.

With their parents working in the fields all day, the children were never washed except at night, and there was no place for them to play except in the dirt. Now Tommy called my attention to Margarita's clean face and hands as he gave her a little bowl of powdered milk and sat down with her while she ate it.

The next morning we were awakened at daybreak by a knock on the door. It was Margarita's father, asking if we had any nails. We knew what that meant, since nails were usually used to build coffins. Someone in the family had died.

Tom and his dog, Johnny Reb, bringing dinner home

Tommy awoke from his cot on the other side of the straw mat we had put up as a wall in our one room, and called to Ken, "Who is it this time, Daddy?" Ken found it difficult to tell him, but finally said, "It was...Margarita, Tom. She died last night." Just a common cold, but her little body was so malnourished that she had no resistance, and overnight she was dead.

It was hard enough for Ken and me to think of the death of this precious little girl we all loved, but it was even harder to see Tommy. He stood there in shock, fighting back his tears. Before we could say any more, he ran out of the house and disappeared into the jungle nearby. It was noon before he came back to face Margarita's death.

Life in the Alto Beni forced our children to grow up much faster than they would have back in Alabama. It also helped them, as well as Ken and me, to develop a global perspective of life and death, and to realize that Christ suffers with us when we are hurting. Through our tears, we thanked God, knowing that He wanted each of us to be a channel for His comfort to flow to those who were suffering.

(opposite page)
Sarah with her large cooking pot, also used for boiling water

A Knock at the Door

*In your unfailing love, you will lead
the people you have redeemed.*
—Exodus 15:13

One who finds it difficult to deviate from a well-planned schedule would be very frustrated living in the Alto Beni. As I have mentioned before, night would often come before we got around to all the tasks we had hoped to accomplish that day. We learned that one of the most important things we could do was to listen to the people who came to our door with some great need. It took a degree of discipline to put out of my mind the chore I was just trying to finish or preparing to begin. Sometimes I could do it without being disturbed; sometimes I couldn't.

One day at 5 A.M., someone knocked at the door. *"Hermana!"* a woman called out in the darkness. I recognized the voice of our neighbor, Ruth. I lit a candle, opened the door and invited her in.

"Hermana, could you possibly take us to Puerto Linares?" she pled. "My brother and his wife have been visiting me and they have tickets on the bus that leaves Puerto Linares this morning. We waited all day yesterday for a truck to pass so we could hitch a ride, but nothing is moving. They're going to miss their bus, and then they won't get to La Paz in time to go back to work. They could lose their jobs!"

"Ruth, no truck has come through because it has been raining again. The road is almost impassable," I explained, as patiently as I could manage. "You know how dangerous it is to cross the mountain along the river. Part of the road has caved in already. We can't risk driving over that unstable ground. Besides, the jeep is not running. We need a part and have to wait till someone comes from La Paz to bring it."

I could not help being relieved that I had a valid reason for not taking the jeep over that treacherous road. Still, I felt for Ruth and her relatives. I, too, had passed through similar experiences before we got the *mobilidad.*

Another Knock at the Door

I started breakfast after Ruth left, but before we could sit down to cat, a young man whom I had not seen before was knocking at our door. "Please, could you buy some corn? We had a good harvest this year, but there is no one to buy it. We heard you had a feed mill and that you are trying to experiment with balanced animal food. Could you please buy our corn? We have no place to keep it and it's so damp, it's soon going to ruin...then all our work will be in vain."

How well I knew the problem of marketing their produce. Last year one homesteader donated hundreds of pounds of tomatoes to feed the fish because there was no *mobilidad* that he could hire to take them to market in time. Every year thousands of dollars worth of hard work was lost to the homesteaders because markets to sell their produce were not available in the Alto Beni, and transportation to take it to other towns and villages was sporadic.

"How much corn do you have?"

"Twenty-five *quintales,* already shelled."

I cringed. A *quintal* was 100 pounds. He had shelled 2500 pounds...by hand!

"CENATEC's feed mill has a corn-sheller on it. You don't ever have to shell corn you want to sell us."

"Ah-h-h!!" He shook his head in disbelief. "How much time it cost me to shell my corn! But, please, will you buy it anyway?"

We couldn't afford to buy 2500 pounds of corn right now. But the expression on the boy's face was so fearful, yet so hopeful that I began to think: *Maybe we could grind it into meal, teach the people to make cornbread and sell it....*

"My place is on the other side of Palos Blancos," he broke into my thoughts. "Only about twenty miles from here. You have a jeep, so it wouldn't be any problem for you to come get the corn."

Oh, if he only knew! To travel twenty miles over a nearly impassable road, where we'd surely get stuck several times and risk sliding off down deep precipices.... He was so crushed with the fear of losing his season's work, however, that he could not see his problem from my point of view. But since the jeep was temporarily out of service, there was no other answer for him.

"I'm so sorry!" I really was. "If you could hire a truck to bring the corn to us, we'll buy it. But our jeep won't run now, so we can't go get it." He left, still hopeful, still fearful. Could he find a *mobilidad?* If there was not a truck, the twenty-mile trip was just as big an obstacle as the two hundred miles to the capital was for one *hermano* who had given us two tons of avocados for fish food since he had no transportation.

We sat down to a cold breakfast, but had hardly begun to eat when a brother of the church knocked at the door. This man handed us 610 *pesos* from the country of Chili. He had worked there several years ago to save this much money. To keep from spending it, he had kept it in Chilean currency. Now he was faced with an emergency and had to cash it.

"But I can't get to La Paz to the money

changer," he said. "Please keep it for me and when you go, change it for me." We didn't tell him because we were not sure, but we thought that Chile's currency had been de-valued since he had lived there, and now he would receive only part of what it was worth.

Promises, Pigs' Toenails, and Prayer

Our next visitor after breakfast that morning was a woman from Palos Blancos whose husband knew how to make brick. He had signed a contract with Ken several months earlier to build a brick oven at CENATEC. The man had agreed to deliver a certain quantity of brick for a team who were coming in May to help us.

He barely finished half the brick he promised, however. Not only that, but we had to hire someone else to build the oven after he failed to finish it. His problem was alcohol. We had not seen him in weeks, but now that he was sober again, his wife had come to visit, bringing us a hen as a gift and promising us that her husband would be here the next day to finish the work—two months late!

I didn't want to take the hen because I knew

they needed the eggs. But she insisted. "No, Sister, if I keep it, it will die anyway. I had thirty hens, but almost all of them are dead now. So we've been eating them as fast as we can to make use of them before they die."

"How do they die?" I asked, regretting more than ever that I had accepted the hen and put her in with my flock.

"They seem well and then, all of a sudden, they give a squawk and fall dead. They all die that way. No one knows why."

But I knew. Cholera had been attacking the chickens from the zone on the other side of her town, wiping out chickens for miles around. Many people now had lost their main source of protein—eggs.

It had taken us months to build up our flock of thirty chickens. I knew what it meant to care for each sick hen, hoping to gain one more to lay eggs. Now, after all these months, they were laying nine to eleven eggs a day. As I looked at her hen, mingling already with mine, I shivered. Maybe we would soon be returning to those days when we had to walk at least three miles to find as many as three or four eggs for sale. Was the hen contaminated? Would cholera strike our chickens next?

A brother, Maximo, interrupted my dismal thoughts. After thanking the woman again and bidding her good-bye, I turned my attention to Maximo. His wife, Marta, had a three-week-old baby and still didn't have enough energy to get out of bed, he said. He had bought some medicine from a peddler, but he couldn't read the directions because it was in German. Would I please read it and tell him the dosage? I was continually amazed at the people who thought we knew so much more than we did. I studied the German words, but could only make out one of them: *asthma.*

"That's all right, *Hermana,*" he consoled me as I lamented not being able to help him. "Just tell me where I can buy some pig's toenails. That will be just as good."

I had learned not to laugh at local remedies, since they usually had some reasoning behind them. So I asked sincerely, "How do you plan to use pig's toenails?"

"We grind them up and make a tea out of the powder," he said. "It gives a sick person energy."

Well, I wasn't so sure about that. *On the other hand,* I contemplated, *isn't Jello made from cow's hooves? They say Jello contains protein. Perhaps pig's toenails would have protein in them too. These people have surely taught me how to use every tiny resource available.*

Sister Asunta came up while we were talking. "I know someone who has ground pig's toenails—*Hermano* Manuel. I'm sure he would pass you some."

Maximo left to search for pig's toenails for his wife, while Asunta began telling me about her next project. She was leaving for Caranavi, the next town some 90 kilometers away, to have her rice milled and sold. I felt so sorry that she had to transport her rice so far, because CENATEC had a new rice mill to be operated together with the feed mill, but its motor was broken right now.

"You have to go all the way to Caranavi with your baby?"

"Yes, it will take three days to go there, mill the rice, then sell it and return, but I must. My husband can't take time away from his job."

"Where will you sleep?"

"In the back of the truck we ride in," she explained. "Could you lend me a flashlight? I'll have to tend the baby in the night."

I might not be able to translate directions on a medicine bottle from German to Spanish, or provide transportation to Puerto Linares, or buy

2500 pounds of corn or change Chilean money to Bolivian—but I could at least loan a sister a flashlight. Relieved to find something I could do to help, I hurried to find it for her.

◊

The needs of the Alto Beni are many and varied, spiritual as well as physical. After Asunta left, another sister came to ask us to pray for her teenage daughter, whom she had sent to study in La Paz. After all her parents' sacrifice, the girl had become rebellious, had quit studying and had failed her course. "May I send her to stay a week here at your mission?" the mother asked. "Maybe your daughters would have a good influence on her."

We prayed with the sister and agreed that her daughter could spend a week with us. Shortly after she left, a twenty-year-old indigenous youth, desperately seeking his place in this world, came to our doorstep. With little education and no land, he did not know where to turn. From his viewpoint, things appeared hopeless. We talked and prayed with him, trying to encourage him, but also realizing that in the jungle, there were few answers for one with little formal education and so few skills.

As the young man left, *Hermano* Martin approached our yard with a big load on his back. He put it down and opened the blanket to reveal fifty pounds of yuca, an edible root similar to potatoes. He had carried his heavy burden down the mountain for nearly an hour.

"How much is your yuca?" I offered to buy some.

"Nothing, Sister. I could not accept money from you. Last Sunday, you gave my wife seven vitamin pills, remember?"

With no pharmacy in Sapecho, one could not buy vitamins or other medicines. So we tried to keep some basic items on hand for emergencies. "Seven vitamins for fifty pounds of yuca? No, *Hermano!* I'll have to send her some more vitamins then."

The spirit of sharing was widespread in Sapecho. Things were not given as a hand-out. They were shared and later the favor was returned. Our neighbors offered us bananas, citrus fruit, rice and chocolate. We gave them vitamins, iron tablets and medicines. This enabled everyone to maintain their sense of dignity and respect for each other.

I sometimes feel as if I have lived a hundred lifetimes—just knowing and feeling the struggle my neighbors experienced. After all, maybe this was the main thing we accomplished during our sojourn in this country. We were a presence for Jesus...someone who listened and cared.

The Ministry of Presence

One of the things I enjoyed most in Sapecho was visiting the people in their homes. Even though many of them were extremely poor and could not read or write, they were most intelligent, resourceful and had so much to teach us.

Even though it took lots of time and energy to reach the homes scattered over the countryside, it was in those homes that we felt the indigenous people really opened up and shared their lives with us on a deeper level. That is where we began to understand their minds and their hearts...and became one with them.

One principle became evident to us. The greatest gift we can give our brothers and sisters living in difficult places and circumstances is to be a presence among them, experience life with them, listen to their joys and sorrows, their disappointments and their dreams and share our own. This is the Ministry of Presence.

Instead of serving in a specific job—such as starting a church, a hospital, a school or teaching, pastoring or attending the sick—we felt that God had called us to become one with the people we had been sent to serve, living on their economic level as much as possible. By participating in their daily lives, we began to understand their needs on a different level. In seeing the potential in the people that they could not see for themselves, and reflecting it back to them, we found that we could become a catalyst for helping them to change.

Sarah, writing in her journal, in her little bamboo home in Sapecho

Last Days in the Alto Beni

We were very happy when a church doctor in the Altiplano, came to help us for a day and a half. He found most of the people to be anemic or suffering from some kind of malnutrition. Most of them did not look starved, for they got calories from such things as rice and bananas, but their bodies could not resist simple diseases, sometimes even such things as a common cold, because of lack of protein, iron and certain vitamins.

Maximo and Marta and their three children had been sickly ever since they moved to our town about six months ago. While the doctor was in the Alto Beni, he examined them. "This family won't survive more than three months more if they don't get iron tablets right away," he declared.

The doctor left a large bottle of iron tablets to be given to those in need. But the homesteaders insisted on paying for them. Even the poorest wanted to pay what they could, in order for us to have money to buy more tablets when those were gone. Maximo came to buy the iron for his three children.

"You need some for yourself and Marta too," I reminded him. "Remember, the doctor said you must have them if you are to live!"

"Yes, Sister," he answered gravely. "I'll get them later."

"You need them now, Maximo," I insisted. "Take enough for all of you and pay for them whenever you can."

"No, Sister," he replied. "I can't make a debt. I might die before I get it paid." No amount of urging could convince him to take them without paying.

"Don't worry about us," he tried to reassure me. "I have a little more rice left from the harvest. I'll sell it this week. I expect to get one hundred pesos for it…(the equivalent of five U.S. dollars). Next week I can buy iron tablets for Marta and me."

The next Sunday Maximo was present when we told the congregation that this would be our last Sunday. For some time, Ken had been having problems with a lump that had kept growing. When he consulted a doctor in La Paz, he was told that he should return to the States for treatment at once. "We fear this might be cancer, and we are not used to treating the disease," he was told. "You should go to a doctor in your own country."

After church, Maximo came to our house and handed me the 100-peso bill that he had received for his last bag of rice. I knew he would have no more income till the next harvest several months from now.

"Maximo, I'm so glad you are getting these iron tablets before we leave," I said as I reached for the bottle of tablets.

"No, Sister," he explained. "This money is not for iron tablets. This is to help Pastor Ken get well."

"But Ken will get well," I objected. "He's going to the States to a doctor. But if you don't take these iron pills, you won't be alive when we get back."

Maximo looked away wistfully. "Yes, Sister," he responded. "But it's a long way to your country and your money might give out before you get there. If I die, my death will affect only my family. But if the Pastor doesn't get well, it will affect all of us."

When I continued to refuse his money, tears came into his eyes, and he said, "Are you denying me the joy of doing what I know I should do?"

I knew I had to take the money. I put it in the box to buy more iron tablets, but Maximo never knew.

I took iron tablets to the man in the church who led the congregation when the pastor wasn't there. "Give these to Maximo," I said to him. "Don't tell him where they came from. Just tell him they were left over from someone else's treatment. They have already been paid for and are not needed. They are going to be wasted, so he must take them."

Finally, under those conditions, Maximo accepted them. And I don't think that I really was untruthful, for those iron tablets were left over from the treatment of love Maximo had graciously given to us. Maximo, his wife Marta, and two older children survived. It was too late for the youngest one. She died of anemia.

$$\Diamond$$

As we were preparing to leave, eighteen-year-old Robin Warnes, one of our Learn and Serve Team members, made the decision not to return to the States with us. We had only recently received the jeep for the Sapecho Church. There was no one in Sapecho who could drive it except Benjo, and he was far too busy to be a full-time chauffeur. The *hermanos* asked Robin to stay and drive the jeep for them to take the sick to the clinic across the river or to other seminars and services.

We did not want to leave the Alto Beni, but

Ken's health was a priority, so we began the final preparations for our trip home. First, though, I needed to see about my aching tooth.

Ken could not take me to a dentist because he would be teaching a three-day course on growing fish for seventy homesteaders who had signed up. Since we would soon be leaving, it was more important than ever that the people learn everything Ken could teach them. Although we hoped to return to the Alto Beni, we had no idea when...or if...we would really be able to come back to this place we had called home for over a year. The thought was depressing.

But at the moment, I needed to find some relief for my throbbing jaw. I had already seen a dentist, who had pulled my wisdom tooth the week before in the capital city. The dentist had apologized because he had no medicine to deaden the pain. I was hurting so badly, I asked him to go ahead and pull the tooth anyway. However, when he tried to pull it, the roots broke off inside the gum and had to be cut out, leaving my jawbone exposed. After returning to Sapecho and spending a week of hard-to-sleep nights and pain-filled days, I decided the time had come to seek further help.

Taking our *mobilidad,* Karen, Robin Warnes and I drove the 75 kilometers from Sapecho to Caranavi. To my dismay, when we arrived, we found that the two dentists in town were away.

The heat of the day was stifling, and we were stressed from the dangerous drive and disappointed not to find a dentist. I suggested to the girls that we get some ice cream at the little open-air parlor in town, the only place this side of La Paz that sold ice cream. It was the second time in a year we had had such luxury.

Winter, which was summer in North America, had passed. The heat once again was intense. It felt like a giant blanket covering us, at times almost suffocating us. I couldn't complain about the heat that day, however. Knowing that we would soon be leaving this area and the people we had come to love caused me to see everything through a new lens. It would not be the Alto Beni without the crushing heat.

I sat there in that little restaurant along the dusty street, soaking up the strangling heat, enjoying every second of it now, knowing that these memories would soon be tucked away in a box of old photographs, to be cherished and prayed over in all the years to come.

At that moment, a little indigenous girl peered through the lattice-work wall at our ice cream. We motioned to her to join us. Surprised and pleased, she sat down beside us and began to eat the pineapple ice cream she had chosen.

"I like coconut best," I told her, and treasured her shy smile along with the heat that made us gasp for breath.

Hot and sweaty, struggling with pain in my gum and unable to find a dentist, I knew that this was only a small taste of the suffering the people lived with daily, trying to find a better life for their children.

Oh, God! I prayed silently. *Thank You! Thank You! I'm glad—so glad—that You have given us this year to live with these precious people.*

That day—one of my last before returning to Alabama—would always live in my memory. Somehow I could not believe that it was time to end our life here together. *Please, God, heal my husband...and, please, let us come back to the Alto Beni!*

◊

Epilogue

Three months after our arrival back home, Ken was well again, and we returned to finish living out our two years in the Alto Beni as we had promised. I hope sometime I can tell you the story of that second wonderful year that taught us even more and bound us even closer to the people of Sapecho.

During those two years, all six of us changed beyond any telling of it. Ken, our children and I know that the thread of a dream we followed to Bolivia has grown and grown and wrapped around us, binding each of us forever to that country.

Looking back, we see that the mot successful part of our ministry was not the projects, even though they helped many people. The greatest part was the changed lives, the changed way of thinking—both in the Bolivians and in ourselves. God met us at the point where we became one with each other. Now, after thirty years, what remains to us are the people, the memories of the life we shared, the tremendous lessons and some fundamental concepts—both technical and spiritual—which we learned from one another.

It is our prayer that those who are reading this book will also remember the people of the Alto Beni—along with more than half the world's population who live in similar conditions—and pray for them regularly. Perhaps God will lead you, as He led us, to make a difference in the life of some needy person or community. It could be as far away as the jungles of Bolivia...or as near as your next-door neighbor.

As I write the final words of this book at my breakfast table back home in the United States, beside me is a to-do list that I must tackle before this day is over....

- Daily household chores
- Milk cow
- Feed chickens
- Respond to letters and emails
- Teach seminar at SIFAT
- Bake birthday cake for Kathy
- Translate for the doctor's visit for migrant worker
- Finish the article for the *SIFAT Journal*...

Oh, excuse me just a minute! Someone is knocking at my door...

SIFAT: Sharing the Love of God in Practical Ways

When the Corsons returned from Bolivia, they knew they had to do something more in response to the experiences that Sarah has written about in this book. Others joined them in 1979 to help establish SIFAT (Servants in Faith and Technology). SIFAT is approved as an Advance Special of the United Methodist Church, and is interdenominational in service, board of directors, staff, and those who participate in the programs. Located in Lineville, Alabama, it is a center to train Christian leaders to empower their communities to develop spiritually and materially. SIFAT's graduates have come from 87 countries to study appropriate technologies for solutions to basic human needs…such as

- water purification
- food production and preservation
- alternative energies
- microenterprise
- prevention of sickness and death in children
  and much more...all in the context of the
  integrated Gospel.

The SIFAT campus has a realistic Global Village where they open a window on the world for literally thousands of American children and youth. There are week-long Learn and Serve mission camps and one-day camps in the CARES program. Many begin to understand why so many people are poor and how everyone can be a part of the solution to hunger and poverty. Hundreds of adults have gone on SIFAT teams to learn and to serve under SIFAT graduates in places like Bolivia, Ecuador, Uganda, and Zambia on short-term teams for long term development. SIFAT invites you to visit and to participate in training events, tours, youth camps or a team to make a real difference among some of the poorest people on our planet.

For more information on SIFAT email www.sifat.org
or call 256-396-2015.

<u>Sponsors:</u>

Rev. Bob and Betty Parris

Harold Harmon

John Harmon

Horace and Mary Jane Sanders

Dr. William and Virginia Brawner

Peggy Walker

Karen Corson

Ken Corson

Gracias to all those who made the publication of
this book possible.